ENGLISH FOR INTERNATIONAL
TOURISM

T0346220

LOUIS HARRISON

CONTENTS

1 SELLING DREAMS

UNIT MENU

Grammar: tense review
Vocabulary: describing locations
Professional skills: marketing
Case study: tour profit margins

1 Read the text and complete the table.

Date	Event
1980s	companies like [1]_____ founded
late [2]_____	the [3]_____ bubble burst
now	more than [4]_____ of sales online

2 Choose the correct verbs to complete the text.

A short history of e-tourism

The potential of the internet for the tourist market [1]*was realized / realized* quickly by entrepreneurs. Companies such as lastminute.com [2]*were launched / have been launched* in the 1980s to fill vacant rooms by providing late booking at low cost. When the dot.com bubble burst in the late 1980s, many internet tourism companies [3]*didn't survive / haven't survived*. However, since then the value of the internet in tourism [4]*has been proved / proved* – in Europe, over 33 % of travel and tourism sales [5]*are now done / are now doing* online.

3 Complete the text with the correct form of the verbs in brackets.

E-tourism

Since the early days of the industry, tourism professionals [1]_____(try) to find better ways of reaching their customers. A good way of doing this is online, but where on the World Wide Web [2]_____customers _____ (spend) their time? Recent research has provided some answers. Over the last few years, the time spent on social media sites [3]_____ (rise) dramatically. Today, social media functions [4]_____ (integrate) into tourism sites like TripAdvisor.com, so often the search for a holiday [5]_____ (start) when customers ask people in their social network for advice. This means less time on the websites of individual travel companies.

Reviews posted online by customers are the most trusted form of advertising. Over the past few years, replying to these reviews [6]_____ (identify) by customer service teams as an area of real importance.

Once, the internet [7]_____ (use) mainly at home, but soon there will be more mobile internet users than desktop users. This means that quite often the customer [8]_____ already _____ (travel) when they get their information. The development of mobile apps, mobile websites and QR codes is essential if the industry is to meet market needs.

PRONUNCIATION

4))) **1.1** Listen to the verb endings and write /t/, /d/ or /id/ according to the final sound.

1 realized __/d/__   2 launched _____   3 survived _____   4 proved _____

5 integrated _____   6 reached _____   7 provided _____   8 started _____

5))) Listen again and practise.

6 Read Lucy's email to her office and decide who she should market the destination to.

Choose the correct option.

a adventure tourists
b cruise tourists
c wedding tourists

From:	Lucy@Balitours.com
To:	Joe@Balitours.com
Subject:	Research update

Dear Joe,

I'm in Bali at the moment, checking out new destinations for next year's tours. It really is a ¹ *snow-capped / tropical* paradise. In the north is the ² *unspoiled / clear-blue* tranquillity of Mount Agung, which is an ideal ³ *off-the-beaten-track / romantic* destination for long-distance hiking and wild camping. After the camping and hiking trip we can take backpackers and travellers to Denpasar in the south, with its clear ⁴*blue / isolated* sea and ⁵ *spectacular / secluded* surfing on Kuta beach. I'll video-call you when I've looked at family holidays.

Regards,

Lucy

7 Read the email again and choose the correct adjective.

8)))) **1.2** Listen to Lucy's video call to the office and tick (✓) the places on the map she recommends.

9)))) Listen again and correct the mistakes in the notes below.

<u>Notes on Lucy's video call</u>
Bali – an ugly Indonesian island
1 adventure tourists – hiking and camping on Mount Batur, but visiting Mount Batur can be peaceful as it's an active volcano. View of dirty Lake Batur at the bottom. Get there by car along winding roads. Lots of comfortable villages to visit.
2 family holidays – near crowded beach at Lovina. Lovina a good mix of accommodation, from B&Bs to luxury hotels with tiny rooms.

10 Complete the brochure with the words and phrases in the box.

> reasonably-priced   second   stunning
> tropical   truly   white sand

New tours to Bali
Get away from it all with your family to the unspoiled island of Bali.

Our Bali tour to the ¹_____ inspiring resort of Lovina with its ²_____ view over the Bali Sea includes ³_____ accommodation just minutes from ⁴ _____ beaches.

Adventurous tourists can enjoy the ⁵ _____ forests leading up to Mount Batur, the active volcano. You'll find that driving along Bali's winding roads is an experience ⁶_____ to none!

1 SELLING DREAMS

1 Read the first part of the article and choose true (T), false (F) or no information (NI).

1 The marketing mix is something companies often get wrong.   T / F / NI

2 The 'four Ps' were developed to clarify the marketing mix.   T / F / NI

3 The 'four Ps' is the only marketing mix model.   T / F / NI

The Marketing Mix

When a company gets its marketing mix wrong, it can be disastrous. The 'marketing mix', or 'four Ps', is the combination of elements that make up your product and it is at the heart of any business. 'The four Ps' were developed in 1960 as a way of defining the elements of the marketing mix and today it is the most widely accepted model of the marketing mix.

2 Read the next part of the article and complete the lower half of the diagram.

Product Marketing Mix

Product	Pricing	Promotions	Placement

+

1_____   2_____   3_____

Services Marketing Mix

The Extended Marketing Mix

While 'the four Ps' is the standard model, it can be extended to 'the seven Ps', the additional 'Ps' being more specific to service industries.

One of the things that defines 'service industry' is people. In a restaurant or hotel, your chef or front desk define you for your customer and they need to make a good impression. This is why service companies spend a lot of money training their staff in customer service.

For our next 'P', let's take a very successful chain of restaurants – Snackway. Its success is partly based on quick service to the customer without a loss in quality, time and time again. It is successful because of its strong processes, which deliver a quality product quickly and repeatedly, showing that process is central to a service industry marketing mix. The final added element is also very important: physical layout. Although services are intangible, tangible elements often come with them to create a good customer experience. Take the example of two hotels: both offer the same service but one has a nice atmosphere, well-dressed staff and music in the background. The other doesn't. Which would you choose?

3 Read the article again and match the questions below with the additional 'Ps'.

a Is the service environment clean? _____

b Am I greeted pleasantly _____

c Is the service of good quality? _____

d Do I like being here? _____

e Did I receive the service when it was promised? _____

f Are the staff paying attention? _____

4 Read the article again and answer the questions.

1 Why are three more Ps sometimes added?

2 Why do service companies spend money on customer service training?

3 Which elements of Snackway's process create a good customer experience?

4 Which of these is a tangible element? Choose the correct option.

a the efficiency of the front desk

b the way the furniture is arranged

c the manner of the receptionist

1 Read the brochure and choose the correct options.

1 Who is the party for?

a young married couples

b young men before they get married

c families

2 What is the total cost for a group of 12 people?

a £2100

b £2160

c £2120

3 The cost of the trip always includes:

a quick entry to a club

b a sightseeing tour

c a driving activity.

A stag party you'll never forget

A *Stagtour's* Amsterdam bachelor party can be as active or as easy-going as you like.

In Amsterdam's laid-back cultural atmosphere you'll be surprised how much this cosmopolitan city has to offer.

Relax and let us organize your last weekend as a single man.

Our Amsterdam stag weekend includes:

* pre-booked hotel and airport transfer, saving you time and money
* guest-list club entry
* optional sightseeing tours of the canals or Ajax football stadium
* guided shopping tour with your own personal shopping consultant
* optional Grand Prix Karting Event

With *Stagtours*, you can be certain your Amsterdam bachelor weekend will be unforgettable and completely stress free!

And all for £180 per person!

2 Read the brochure again and find:

1 one word meaning *from many different countries*

_____

2 one word meaning *something you will remember*

_____

3 three words/phrases meaning

relaxed _____; _____; _____

3 Read the invoices and decide which part of the tour A–F was the most expensive.

A

Invoice from ***Northern Charter Planes***
to Stagtour
Return flight Manchester to Amsterdam

| £44.50 per person | 12 people | £534 |

B

Invoice
Airport Shuttle >>>>
Hotel transfer for Stagtour bachelor group

£12.50 per person: £150

C

Invoice
Amsterdam Canal Tours

| Canal tour | £10 per person | 12 people | £120 |

D

Invoice
★STADIUM TOURS★

| £15 per person | 5 people | £75 |

E

Invoice
Vondelpark Hotel
Twin room plus breakfast

Two nights at £45 per night per person
with 20% discount   £972

F

Invoice
Escape Nightclub
Invoice for Stagtour group

£15 per person;
10% group (of 12) booking discount   £162

4))) **1.3** Listen to Eve and Matt discussing the costs of the weekend break and correct the invoices they think are wrong.

5))) Listen again and answer the questions.

1 Do Eve and Matt think their profit margin is good at first?

2 Why was the tour invoice wrong?

3 Why was the hotel invoice wrong?

4 What do they calculate their profit margin to be at the end?

5 What are they going to do?

2 GETTING THERE

1 Read the text below and decide which tips answer questions a–c.

a Is there food and drink on the train? _____

b Are the trains reliable? _____

c How do I reserve a seat? _____

3 Complete the final tip with the words and phrases in the box.

> bedding   class   compartments
> power sockets   seats

Tips for train travel in India

1 Your reservation

India's reservation system is easy and convenient. Your ticket has your train, coach and berth number on it. The reservation list is on the door of the train carriage.

2 Refreshments

There are no restaurants on board Indian trains but an attendant will ask you if you would like to order food. An hour later they will return with food from the train's kitchen.

3 Timekeeping

When trains in India are late, they are really late – but generally, the network is very efficient.

4 Coaches

Go for First ^1_____ Air-conditioned as all these coaches have ^2_____ for individual travellers or families. There are ^3_____ for your electrical equipment, with ^4_____ near the windows for daytime travel and berths with ^5_____ for when you're ready to sleep.

2 Read the article again and find words which mean:

1 one of the parts of a train where passengers sit _____

2 a place for someone to sleep in a ship or on a train _____

3 carried on a ship, plane, car, etc. _____

4 someone whose job is to look after or help customers in a public place _____

5 a system of lines, tubes, wires, roads, etc that cross each other and are connected to each other _____

4))) 2.1 Listen to Linda ask her colleague for travel advice from Edinburgh to London and choose the correct answers.

1 Heather didn't fly because the flight

   a was cancelled

   b left too early in the morning

   c wasn't cheap enough.

2 She didn't drive because

   a she felt sleepy

   b it's too far to drive in a day

   c the traffic was bad.

3 The journey takes

   a 4

   b 6

   c 8 hours.

5))) Listen again and complete the sentences.

1 Flying was _____ expensive and there were _____ delays.

2 You can avoid the traffic _____ in the city.

3 It's not exactly a _____ service but it's easy and _____ .

4 It's a very low _____ _____ of transport.

6 Read extracts A–C and decide which one comes from:

1 a travel magazine article
2 directions for a car driver
3 a cruise advert

A

How to find us: Take the dual carriageway for two miles until you reach the roundabout. Take the third exit and the Exhibition Centre is on your right. Alternatively, a taxi will drop you off for around £6.

B

The Mediterranean Dream sets off from the harbour at Nice, France. The liner has three decks of comfortable berths. On deck 2, you can exchange money at the purser's office before you go ashore. You'll look forward to sailing with us.

C

Many people complain about UK airports: after you hang around to collect your boarding pass, you have to get through security. This often involves taking off your shoes and unpacking your laptop. Then you have to fight your way to the departure lounge. All this before you even get on the plane and suffer from jet lag at the other end.

7 Read the extracts again and find words and phrases to complete the definitions.

1 A _____ is a raised circular area where three or more roads join together and which cars must drive around.

2 One of the different levels on a ship is called a _____ .

3 A _____ is an area of water next to the land where the water is calm, so that ships are safe when they are inside it.

4 When you go _____ , you go on from a lake, river, sea, etc. towards the land.

5 The place at an airport where people wait until their plane is ready to leave is the _____ .

6 An official card that you have to show before you get onto a plane is a _____ .

7 _____ is the tired and confusing feeling that you get after flying a very long distance.

8 Read the extracts again and find:

1 one three part multi-word verb _____
2 two multi-word verbs with no object _____ ; _____
3 four multi-word verbs with an object _____ _____ ; _____ ; _____

9 Choose the correct multi-word verb to complete the sentences.

1 Could all non-EU passengers _____ their landing cards before arrival?
   a fill in
   b set off
   c hold up
2 When did you _____ that you'd left your passport at home?
   a put up
   b drop off
   c find out
3 Isn't Andrea here yet? We can't _____ for her all morning.
   a turn up
   b take off
   c hang around
4 Alex, I hope your brother doesn't just _____ without telling me.
   a fill in
   b pick up
   c turn up
5 We'll need to _____ early to catch the train.
   a set off
   b get on with
   c get through

PRONUNCIATION

10 Put the words into the correct group according to their stress pattern.

> carriageway   comfortable   compartment
> departure   equipment   expensive   ~~motorway~~
> roundabout   stopover   unpacking

A ● • •   1 _motorway_
          2 _____
          3 _____
          4 _____
          5 _____

B • ● •   1 _____
          2 _____
          3 _____
          4 _____
          5 _____

11))) 2.2 Listen and check. Then listen and practise.

1 Read the article and decide which is the best summary.

a Dealing with complaints

b Disadvantages of mail marketing

c Prioritizing the right customers

Is the customer always right? It depends ...

For years, Apex Travel offered free weekend breaks to people on their mailing list. The idea was that customers would later book a complete holiday with Apex. However, after two years, Apex found that people were getting the benefit of the free holidays but not buying holidays at the full price at a later date. Apex dealt with the situation by cutting their mailing list, thus reducing their 'bad', non-spending customers by 22 %. As a result, Apex were able to focus on their good customers.

Companies must avoid bad customers because they use up resources that can be spent on good customers. Furthermore, bad customers are likely to upset even the most patient staff members by complaining frequently. A bad customer is likely to have come to you through a special offer, discount or other inexpensive way of getting your product. In the end, they show poor customer loyalty, often switching companies.

Companies need to look after the good customers. When things do go wrong, the customer care team must deal with them with empathy and understanding, and reassure them that it will put things right immediately. Remember, these are the customers who will buy from you again and again. So is the customer always right? The majority are, most of the time.

2 Read the article again and answer the questions.

1 How did Apex hope to sell full-priced holidays?

2 What were people not doing?

3 How did Apex reduce the customers who didn't buy their products?

4 How do companies attract bad customers?

5 Why should companies try to keep good customers?

3 Find words and phrases in the article to match the definitions.

1 an advantage, improvement or help that you get from something _____

2 to give special attention to a person or thing _____

3 able to wait calmly for a long time or to accept difficulties _____

4 the process of looking after people who buy your goods or services _____

5 to make someone feel calmer and less worried about a problem _____

4 Complete the advice card with words from the article.

Apex customer care team advice card

Look after good customers!

1 Treat good customers with _____ to show you understand their needs.

2 If something is wrong, reassure the customer that you will _____ it _____ at once.

Beware of bad customers!

3 Look at how they use up your _____ .

4 Note how often they _____ to staff.

5 Research how frequently they _____ between companies.

---

1 Read the newspaper extracts and tick (✓) the problems that are mentioned.

    1 dealing with air rage / poorly behaved passengers _____

    2 long queues _____

    3 poor in-flight food _____

    4 extra charges _____

    5 staff shortages _____

    6 uncomfortable seating _____

Budget airline told to be more transparent

When does a £20 ticket to Ibiza not cost £20? When you book it through CheapSky Airlines. Air travellers are complaining about the hidden costs of booking with CheapSky: from credit card charges to baggage charges to check-in charges. Hidden costs like these make the advertised price of £20 more like £75 per ticket.

MORE SEATS, LESS ROOM

If you're over 1.5 metres tall, don't book a seat with CheapSky Airlines. Yesterday, the budget airline announced they were putting more seats into their planes in order to lower prices. But a quick calculation shows that they have cut legroom and passenger comfort again.

Mind your manners

The Airline Regulator told CheapSky Airlines that discipline wasn't good enough on their planes. Bad mannered passengers were pushing other passengers to get to the plane first and taking all the locker space, causing complaints that the aircrew weren't doing enough to stop the bad behaviour.

2 Read the texts again. Are the statements true (T) or false (F)?

    1 CheapSky make customers pay more when they use a credit card.   T / F

    2 The airline put more seats in the plane and increased the ticket cost.   T / F

    3 Some people are trying to get on the plane before the other passengers.   T / F

    4 The in-flight aircrew weren't trying very hard to stop the bad behaviour.   T / F

3 🔊 **2.3** Alicia, from CSM Customer Service Training, gives a talk to CheapSky Airlines. Listen and complete the table with the correct percentages.

Passengers disliked …	Budget airline	Scheduled airline
uncomfortable seating	1 _____	23 %
too many extras in ticket price	44 %	2 _____
poor in-flight food	3 _____	12 %
bad passenger behaviour	4 _____	11 %
not cheap / too expensive	31 %	5 _____

4 🔊 Listen again. Match the problems 1–5 with the suggestions a–e.

    1 uncomfortable seating

    2 too many extras in ticket price

    3 poor in-flight food

    4 bad passenger behaviour

    5 not cheap enough

    a training to deal with difficult passengers

    b tell passengers about the low fares they get

    c provide a list of charges

    d provide an alternative menu

    e inform passengers that the final price depends on their choices

5 Look at the table in Exercise 3 again and identify the two most serious problems for scheduled airlines.

3 ACCOMMODATION

1 Read the article and tick (✓) the things Jenny Jackson must have when she's staying in a hotel.

1 a penthouse floor _____   **2** organic cotton sheets _____   **3** a sauna _____

4 smartcard access _____   **5** a white room _____

Demanding Diva

Forget the in-room minibar, sauna and fitness centre. Today's favourite celebrity, film and pop star VIP Jenny Jackson, demands much more from her accommodation. Not only does Jenny have a large entourage when she's on tour, including bodyguards, manager, therapist, voice trainer and personal doctor, she also has very particular personal demands. It's a must that all her people are on the same penthouse floor of the hotel. Access must be smartcard only for security and there should be an executive suite for Jenny to practise in. Inside Jenny's room, it must be exceptionally quiet so she can meditate and there must be white

organic Egyptian cotton bedding and Canadian mineral water at room temperature. If the room is painted white, that's a big plus for the hotel. But her biggest worry is arriving late for the concert: Jenny demands a limousine with police escort to get her there on time.

On vacation, Jenny is more relaxed – she still has her entourage but this time her family and personal chef go, too. Jenny still has demands: her chef cooks vegetarian meals; no CCTV on her floor; pet-grooming service for her four dogs; and certainly no photographers staying in the same hotel.

2 Read the article again and choose the correct answers.

1 Who does Jenny NOT need to have with her? A person or people to:
  a look after her health
  b help with physical exercise
  c protect her

2 Why does Jenny need a quiet room?
  a to paint pictures
  b to record songs
  c to practise meditation

3 Why does she need a police escort?
  a to get to the show on time
  b for security
  c to get home early

4 What does Jenny NOT want on holiday?
  a grooming for her dogs
  b publicity
  c her children

3 Find 12 hotel facilities in the wordsquare. Some are two words or hyphenated words; some are from the text in Exercise 1.

W	A	J	U	U	A	D	E	C	R	X	Y	P	X	I	G	L	U	J	N	K	N	X	A	Y
F	C	J	U	V	F	Y	O	Z	J	R	E	S	T	A	U	R	A	N	T	G	H	J	P	L
H	A	Y	X	U	O	M	C	Z	Y	R	E	S	H	V	X	C	F	B	N	L	O	Z	N	O
P	Q	H	M	Q	P	M	O	F	R	Q	T	G	O	S	K	F	Q	I	A	A	S	Z	H	J
R	D	K	I	Z	H	A	I	R	D	R	Y	E	R	V	Z	S	N	W	M	U	A	W	R	P
A	X	F	I	T	N	E	S	S	C	E	N	T	R	E	U	O	N	C	I	N	T	A	S	U
Z	V	E	I	S	S	J	C	E	Z	P	V	F	Q	R	I	S	E	M	N	D	E	G	M	I
K	I	G	F	C	Z	R	S	C	T	Q	E	T	W	T	F	A	E	M	I	R	L	G	A	I
T	E	F	D	O	R	U	K	I	Q	J	B	T	I	Y	K	U	S	W	B	Y	L	J	R	P
G	U	F	B	M	O	S	H	D	Q	L	Y	D	G	V	T	N	U	U	A	L	I	G	T	O
Q	V	C	O	H	F	T	H	Q	G	B	N	Y	M	R	S	A	D	B	R	T	T	F	C	M
B	L	Y	T	G	W	C	U	J	B	O	Y	Y	C	Z	O	O	H	T	S	I	E	F	A	J
E	L	N	L	C	F	N	A	F	C	W	F	Z	I	X	I	O	W	W	M	B	T	M	R	O
F	E	Q	K	K	E	V	D	R	Z	C	Y	N	Y	L	S	D	M	O	U	M	V	M	D	Z
P	E	W	J	C	K	M	I	L	Q	H	I	L	D	F	G	V	C	I	L	K	A	I	R	H
V	J	I	H	S	Q	A	C	K	V	E	V	E	P	Y	O	C	T	D	N	M	I	I	O	H
Z	N	Z	F	X	J	E	X	E	C	U	T	I	V	E	S	U	I	T	E	G	E	B	O	J

4 Label the picture of a 'capsule' hotel with the words and phrases in the box.

air conditioning
blinds   capsule
control panel
local and satellite TV
locker

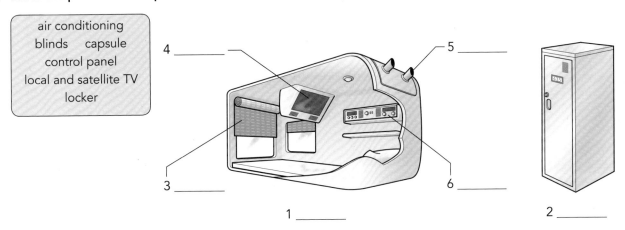

5))) **3.1** Listen to the podcast and decide which two types of customer would use a capsule hotel.

a business people working late

b tourists on a package holiday

c young travellers on a budget

6))) Listen again and complete the information with the correct numbers.

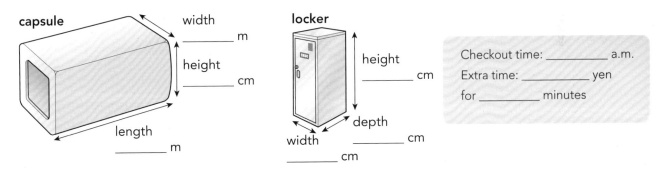

PRONUNCIATION

7))) **3.2** Look at the measurements in Exercise 6. Listen and practise saying them.

8 Choose the correct modal verb to complete the rules.

Capsule hotel rules

A capsule hotel is open 24 hours a day so you [1] *have to / can* book in any time. However, you [2] *mustn't / have to* check out at 10 a.m. or you [3] *must / can* pay an extra 500 yen per 30 minutes.

There is very little room in the capsule, so you [4] *have to / can* store your clothes and belongings in a locker. Men and women [5] *mustn't / don't have to* sleep in the same accommodation sections and visitors [6] *should / may* wear the clothes provided in the locker for reasons of hygiene and comfort.

9 Complete the rules with the modal verbs in the box.

cannot   don't have to   have to   may   must not   should

1 Not allowed: People with tattoos _____ stay.

2 Forbidden: You _____ be noisy.

3 Recommended or advised: You _____ have a massage before sleeping.

4 Necessary: When you enter the hotel, you _____ put your shoes in the shoe locker.

5 Allowed to: We store large items of luggage for you at the front desk, so you _____ leave large items there.

6 Not necessary: You _____ leave at 10 a.m. but you have to pay for the extra time you stay.

1 Read the text and complete the key points 1–5 with the things people can say, a–g.

a 'What seems to have happened is …'

b 'How can we improve the experience you have had with our service?'

c 'Would you mind if I record the problem so that we can make sure it doesn't happen again?'

d 'I'm sorry for the inconvenience – I understand how you feel.'

e 'It's against company policy.'

f 'Your experience is rare and I'm not sure what has happened.'

g 'It's not on our system.'

2))) **3.3** Listen to a conversation and say which is the only key point from the text below that was followed.

Handling customers with complaints

The difference between keeping and losing a customer can sometimes come down to how you deal with their complaint. Here are five key points.

1 Always acknowledge the customer's complaint and apologize for the trouble. Use expressions such as:

_____

2 Ask what the customer would like you to do to make things better for them. Say something like:

_____

3 Don't blame anyone else or your company – let the customer know that it is an exceptional situation _____
If you need to give an explanation, don't be specific; say something like:

_____

4 Write down what the complaint is so your customer knows you are taking action. You could say:

_____

5 Never say _____
or _____
This is the last thing an angry customer wants to hear. Arguing with the customer never works and is bound to make the situation worse.

---

3))) Listen again and choose true (T), false (F) or no information (NI).

1 The customer booked her room less than four weeks ago. T / F / NI

2 The customer has gone to the right hotel. T / F / NI

3 The customer booked her room with a temporary receptionist. T / F / NI

4 The hotel has no other rooms that night. T / F / NI

5 The customer is pleased with the result. T / F / NI

4))) **3.4** Listen to a second version of the same conversation and put the things the receptionist does in the correct order.

_____ say it's an exceptional situation

_____ explain what has happened

_____ apologize for the problem

_____ check back with the customer to make sure they're satisfied

_____ let the customer know you're taking action

5))) Listen to the second version again and choose the words you hear to complete the sentences.

1 I'm _sorry / afraid_ we don't have you booked in tonight.

2 I'll look _at / into_ it right away for you.

3 There seem to _be / have been_ some problems.

4 I've done _everything / all the things_ I possibly can.

5 I'll ask the manager tomorrow to _check / see_ that you were satisfied with your room.

1 Read the email extracts and tick (✓) the things the people complain about in each one.

	A	B	C
1 swimming pool safety	____	____	____
2 hygiene	____	____	____
3 restaurant food	____	____	____
4 lack of hot water	____	____	____
5 laundry	____	____	____
6 being disturbed	____	____	____
7 power supply	____	____	____
8 overpricing	____	____	____

2 Read the extracts again and decide which complaint is the most serious.

A

From:	EvaH@home.com
To:	manager@Hilltop.com
Subject:	Campsite complaint

… our experience at your site was very poor. First of all, we couldn't sleep due to the noise from a group of students outside their tent even though your advert said no noise after 10 p.m. Secondly, the kitchen and the toilets were filthy. Finally, the food at the site restaurant was disgusting and gave my children food poisoning.

B

From:	DavidJ@jmail.com
To:	admin@hotelsplendid.com
Subject:	Complaint

… the bathroom had not been cleaned after the previous guests had left and later we noticed that the bed sheets were dirty. Furthermore, the walls must be made of paper as we could hear the couple next door to us shouting and arguing all night.

C

From:	Luc@tmail.com
To:	manager@Hilltop.com
Subject:	Refund

We would like a refund of the money we spent at your site. The facilities were not as advertised – the electricity went off once at 11 so there was no lighting on site one night. There was a lot of noise from other people and, finally, the caravan site toilet facilities were not cleaned regularly.

3 Read the reply and tick (✓) the complaints the manager accepts.

1 noise disturbance _____
2 poor food standards _____
3 poor hygiene _____

Dear Madam,

A I am writing with reference to your complaint of 8th August. First of all, I would like to apologize for the problems that occurred during your stay with us.

B We take great care to make sure that our hygiene standards are of the highest quality and that our guests keep noise to a minimum, especially at night. However, on this occasion we have fallen below our usual high standards. This was due to a shortage of personnel.

C Regarding your experience at our restaurant, I'm afraid that we have had no other complaints about this and no other reports of food poisoning, and can only suggest this may have been caused by something you ate outside the restaurant.

D We would like to offer a part refund and hope that you will return again next year.

E I will call you soon to check that this is satisfactory.

Reginald Smith

Site Manager

Hilltop Campsite

4 Read the reply again and match paragraphs A–E with 1–5 below.

1 say you will follow this up ____
2 acknowledge the complaint and apologise for the problem ____
3 suggest a solution ____
4 say this is not normal and give an explanation ____
5 reject part of the complaint and suggest an alternative cause ____

4 DESTINATIONS

1 Match the words and phrases with the weather symbols.

> cloudy   cold front   drizzle   heavy rain
> light rain   light snow   sunny intervals
> thundery showers   tropical storm

1 _____   4 _____   7 _____

2 _____   5 _____   8 _____

3 _____   6 _____   9 _____

2))) 4.1 **Listen to three weather forecasts and match them with the maps below. There is one more map than you need.**

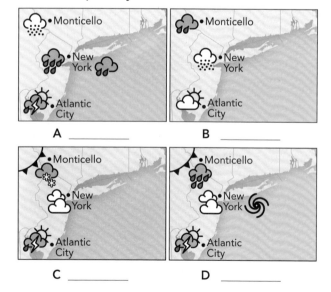

A _____   B _____

C _____   D _____

3))) **Listen again and complete the table with the correct temperatures.**

	New York	Atlantic City	Monticello
Friday	50° F		
Saturday		52° F	
Sunday			35° F

4 Complete the text with the words in the box.

> average   changeable   climate   drought
> extreme   humid   temperate   tropical

New Jersey

Between the Atlantic Ocean and the Delaware River, New Jersey has a moderate [1]_____, with cold winters and warm, wet, [2]_____ summers. In Atlantic City, the [3]_____ temperature is 54° F, ranging from 30° F in January to 75° F in July. In spring and autumn, the weather can be [4]_____, with sunny intervals and sudden showers, but temperatures are not usually really high nor very low – the state has a [5]_____ climate.
Occasionally, the state experiences [6]_____ weather, with hurricanes and [7]_____ storms. Although rainfall is plentiful, a serious [8]_____, or water shortage, occurs on average every 15 years.

5 Read the text and choose the correct words.

Our travel nightmare came true when we were caught by Hurricane Irene while we were travelling to a business meeting. We couldn't [1] *cancel / disrupt* the meeting but at the same time, the storm had [2] *blocked / grounded* all flights from JFK and hundreds of people were [3] *stranded / stood*. We called our business partner to tell her that we would be [4] *delayed / cancelled* and drove inland, where we thought we could be OK. We were at first but as we drove south, the weather got worse. We thought we might get through but a tree had been blown down at Trenton and had [5] *stranded / blocked* the road. So we had to turn back – away from the meeting and towards the storm.

6 Read the text again and answer the questions.
1 Why were flights cancelled?
2 How did they decide to travel eventually?
3 What happened as they went south?
4 What stopped them getting to the meeting?

7 Read the text and label the picture with the correct place name.

Turkey's favourite destinations

1 Istanbul

For anyone visiting Turkey, Istanbul is a must-see city. As the capital of two major empires, the city is full of ancient monuments. When you want to get out of the city, you can take a ferry across the Sea of Marmara to the small archipelago of the Princes' Islands. If you visit in April, you can also catch Istanbul's delightful Tulip Festival.

2 Pamukkale

A short connecting flight from Istanbul to Denizli, then a shuttle bus takes you to the resort of Pamukkale. Here, natural mineral waters pour down the slopes of the hill to form travertines – pools of mineral water. You can bathe in the mineral waters or take a walk in the ruins of ancient Hieropolis.

3 Cappadocia

Situated on [1] <u>the central plateau</u>, [2] <u>Cappadocia</u> is a place of wonder and beauty, its fairy chimneys rising up like towers. Here, you can stay in different types of [3] <u>accommodation</u>, including [4] <u>a cave hotel</u>. In Cappadocia, [5] <u>tourists</u> can visit the fairy chimneys, cave dwellings and underground cities, [6] <u>the best example</u> being Derinkuyu.

_____

8 Read the text again and find words and phrases which mean:

1 buildings or other structures that are built to remind people of an important event or famous person

2 a boat that carries people or goods across a river or a narrow area of water

3 a group of small islands

4 a special occasion when people celebrate something, such as a religious event, and there is often a public holiday

5 to continue a journey by aeroplane after a previous journey by air

6 a plane, bus or train that makes regular short journeys between two places

7 pieces of ground or surfaces that go downwards

8 tall narrow buildings either built on their own or forming part of a castle or church

9 Read the paragraph about Cappadocia again and match rules A–C with underlined examples 1–6.

A Use the indefinite article
to refer to something for the first time _____

B Use the definite article
to refer to a specific or particular thing _____
with superlatives _____

C Use no article before
the names of most cities and countries _____
plural nouns used in a general sense _____
uncountable nouns _____

10 Read the text and choose *a*, *the* or Ø if no article is necessary.

One of [1] *a / the / Ø* most interesting and unusual attractions in [2] *a / the / Ø* Cappadocia are [3] *a / the / Ø* underground cities. There may be up to 40 underground cities, with the most famous being [4] *a / the / Ø* Derinkuyu. Derinkuyu has eight floors, reaching 85 metres below [5] *a / the / Ø* ground. [6] *A / The / Ø* city had schools and storerooms among other places, and between 20,000 and 50,000 [7] *a / the / Ø* people may have lived there. It has an area of at least 650 m² and was connected to the other cities through [8] *a / the / Ø* system of long tunnels.

1)))) 4.2 **Listen to a conversation between a travel adviser and a customer. Are the statements true (T) or false (F)?**

1 Mrs Gee spoke to the travel advisor the previous night about the holiday. T / F

2 The family want to go somewhere cheap. T / F

3 Mr and Mrs Gee are active people. T / F

4 The travel adviser only has a limited range of options for Mr and Mrs Gee. T / F

5 Mr Gee does the cooking at home. T / F

2)))) **Listen again and complete the Customer requirements form.**

Customer requirements form

1 Name   Mrs Denise Gee

2 Duration   ¹_____ weeks

3 Number of people   ²_____

4 Region / Country   Mediterranean coast

5 Price   around ³_____

6 Additional information

Mrs Gee would like a ⁴_____ *holiday but would like to have activities for her* ⁵_____ *A*⁶_____ *is important – possibly at a* ⁷_____ *hotel or holiday village. They enjoy watching movies, somewhere with a* ⁸_____ *would be good, but they may need a* ⁹_____ *service for this. The accommodation must be* ¹⁰_____*catered.*

3 **Complete the email with the words and phrases in the box.**

> advise   could maybe   if I were you
> recommend   why not

Dear Denise,

Following our conversation I can ¹_____ these wonderful holiday destinations.

1 Sassari Hotel Resort

On the beautiful island of Sardinia, the Sassari Hotel Resort has spacious, fully-catered accommodation, an Olympic-sized swimming pool but no childcare service. There are organized sports like windsurfing or volleyball on the hotel's safe private beach. ²_____ relax in the evening at the on-site cinema or disco? ³_____ , I would book well in advance as this resort is very popular. The cost for two weeks would be £3,980.

2 Paphos Holiday Village

This safe family holiday village offers fully-catered accommodation on the spectacular Cyprus coast. There are activities for all ages: you ⁴_____ take your children swimming (the pool has water chutes), go riding at the equestrian centre or go on a turtle-spotting tour. Childcare services are available so you can enjoy the evening entertainment. Again, I ⁵_____ you to book early as this is a popular destination and a bargain at £3,100 for two weeks.

4 **Decide which holiday is better for Denise.**

5 **Read the email again and find words which mean:**

1 a place where a lot of people go for holidays

2 large, with plenty of space to move around in

3 not in danger of being harmed, lost, or stolen

4 a place where you can ride a horse

5 a reptile that lives mainly in water and has a soft body covered by a hard shell

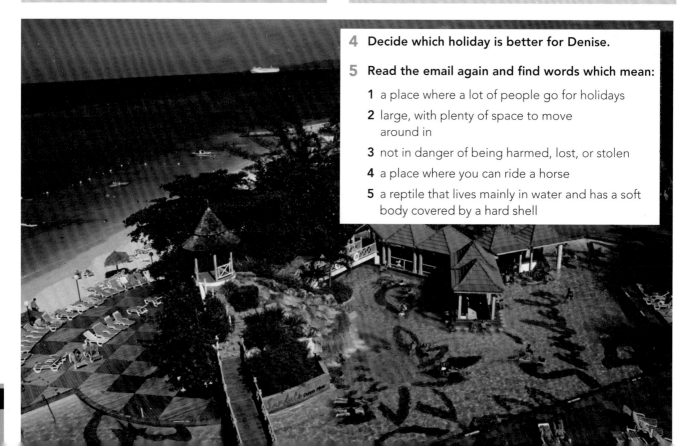

1 Read the report and tick (✓) the true sentences.

  1 Jamaica has a long tradition of good music. _____

  2 Jamaican tourism is focused on beach holidays. _____

  3 The tourism sector has earned over $2 billion so far this year. _____

  4 There was a decline in tourism in other Caribbean countries. _____

  5 The tourist sector accounts for 25 % of the economy. _____

Jamaica is justly famous for its beaches, rich musical heritage and tropical climate. The island has plenty to offer tourists inland, with spectacular mountains, forests and rivers as well as interesting towns and colonial-style cities, such as the capital, Kingston. Jamaica also has well-established resorts: Montego Bay, Ocho Rios and Negril. In spite of social problems caused by unemployment and a high murder rate, the tourism sector is on target to earn around $2.06 billion this year, compared with $1.97 billion last year. Jamaica has seen good growth from this sector recently, with 1.76 million tourists last year, increasing to 1.83 million this year. This is in contrast with other Caribbean countries which saw falls in tourism this year. Tourism represents around one fifth of Jamaica's income and is very important for employment, with jobs in tourism rising from last year's 35,257 to 36,321 today. But not everyone is happy – environmental activists warn that relying too heavily on tourism is damaging the country's natural resources and unbalancing the economy.

2 Read the report again. Match the charts with the words in the box and fill in the numbers for Chart C.

Employment   Revenue   Visitors

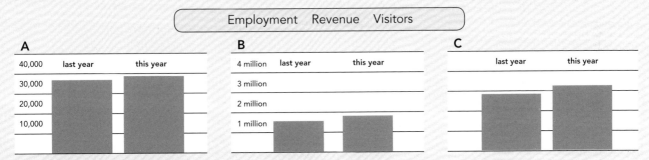

PRONUNCIATION

3))) **4.3** **Listen and choose the large number in each pair that you hear.**

  1 a 120　　　**b** 1,200　　　　**4 a** 1,830,000　　　**b** 183,000

  2 a 35,257　　**b** 35,321　　　　**5 a** 1,790,000,000　**b** 1,700,900,000

  3 a 8,250　　　**b** 825,000　　　　**6 a** 1,500,000　　　**b** 1,500,000,000,000

4))) **Listen again and practise.**

5))) **4.4** **Listen to a TV debate and choose the correct words to complete the sentences.**

  1 Ms Rodney is an expert on *the economy / the environment / the government.*

  2 The new resorts will cost *$5.5 million / $15 million / $5.5 billion.*

  3 Jamaica's other industries are *growing / shrinking / not developing or declining.*

  4 The income from tourism can be used to
  develop eco-tourism / develop power and water supplies / cut the murder rate.

6))) **Listen again and complete the SWOT analysis.**

Strengths: experienced ¹ _____ ; ² _____ tourist industry	Weaknesses: inefficient ³ _____ network for electricity and ⁴ _____ supplies
Opportunities: increase ⁵ _____ projects	Threats: long-term: competition from ⁶ _____ places, e.g. Cuba; short-term: ⁷ _____ , which causes social unrest; high ⁸ _____ rate

UNIT MENU

Grammar: conditional structures with *if*
Vocabulary: geographical features, describing activities, attractions, works of art
Professional skills: speaking to a group
Case study: plan a coach tour

1 Read the visitor profiles and say which people:

a want to take advantage of the exchange rate

b will stay only two days

c are on a limited budget

> **1**
> Suleyman is very keen on art and wants to visit Berlin on a weekend city break.

> **2**
> Jeff and Jacqui are backpacking and want to see as much as possible but spend as little as possible in one day.

> **3**
> The Swedish krone is very strong against the euro, and Sven and Agnes are keen to find some shopping bargains.

2 Read the brochure and complete it with the phrases in the box.

> a great day out   be sure   check out
> famous for   starting point   take advantage

One of Europe's major capitals, Berlin has something for everyone

A Get stranded on Museum Island

Museum Island has two of Berlin's most important museums. ¹_____ to see the Pergamon Museum – this major archaeological museum is always worth visiting.

B Walk – and grab a bargain – in Mauerpark

Mauerpark is ²_____ its massive flea market, which is packed with people selling affordable clothes, bicycles, food, musical instruments and furniture.

C Two wheels or four?

For a fun and cheap way to see many of the major sites, hire a bike. But if a cycle tour isn't for you, enjoy ³_____ on a Trabi-safari, where you tour the city in an old East German car, complete with a lively audio guide.

3 Look at the brochure again and decide which attractions and activities in A–E are good for the visitors in Exercise 1. Some visitors will enjoy more than one attraction.

4 Find words and phrases in the brochure which mean:

1 a place which is very interesting to go to and spend time at _____

2 not at all expensive _____   _

3 extremely full of people _____

4 someone who has a lot of energy and is very active _____

5 enjoyable and amusing _____

6 something which is worth the price you pay for it _____

D Friedrichstrasse

Full of designer shops and other retail outlets, Friedrichstrasse is the place to ⁴_____ of the huge range of shopping destinations. Make sure you ⁵_____ Europe's biggest department store KaDeWe. For value for money, try Moritzplatz.

E Visit Bauhaus Museum

The birthplace of modern design is the Bauhaus Museum – the perfect ⁶_____ for a cultural tour of Berlin.

5 Read the article about Kazakhstan and tick (✓) the activities you can do there.

1 __ 2 __ 3 __ 4 __ 5 __ 6 __ 7 __ 8 __

Kazakhstan

Crossing two time zones, the ninth largest country in the world has a rich and varied landscape, containing deserts, grassy plains, wild forests, spectacular lakes, mountains and glaciers.

With two thirds of the country plains and desert in the west, it's a great chance to experience the nomadic life. In fact, why not have some adventure and go horse-riding across the plains and stay overnight in a yurt? In the south-east of the country, just half an hour from the old capital, Almaty, are mountain ranges and glaciers. If you're a skiier or climber, you'll find all the excitement you want in Tien Shan – the 'Heaven's mountains'. The beautiful rivers running down from the mountains create dramatic waterfalls on their way to inland seas like the Aral or Caspian Sea. If you're looking for water sports, you should go whitewater rafting on the Turgen river. Alternatively, if you're a nature lover, you'll find a wide variety of wildlife and can enjoy activities like watching birds. Or you might like to take a boat out on the Caspian Sea and try your luck at catching fish.

6 Complete the definitions with words from the text.

1 _____ are large areas of land where it is always very hot and dry, and there is a lot of sand.

2 _____ are places where water from a river or stream falls down over a cliff or rock.

3 Large masses of ice which move slowly down a mountain valley are called _____ .

4 Mountain _____ are groups of mountains, usually in a line.

5 _____ are large areas of flat dry land.

7 Use the correct pairs of verbs in the box to complete the first conditional sentences.

arrive / take   love / enjoy   not see/stay   travel / reach   visit / be   want / go

1 You _____ the buildings in Astana – the new capital – if you _____ modern architecture.

2 If you _____ the plains, you _____ able to stay in a yurt.

3 You _____ the national day celebrations if you don't _____ tonight.

4 If you _____ east, you _____ the border with China.

5 If Gengis _____ to go hunting with eagles, he should _____ to Nura.

6 You _____ at Almaty sooner if you _____ the bus.

8 Match sentences 1–4 with a–d.

1 You like old architecture. a The Hotel Superior suits him.

2 Steven wants luxury accommodation. b You have to hurry up.

3 You want to catch the next train. c He doesn't serve you quickly next time.

4 You don't give the waiter a tip. d You enjoy Almaty.

9 Make first conditional sentences from the sentences you matched in Exercise 8. Begin with *If* and change the verb forms as necessary.

1 **Match the comments 1–5 with the tips A–E in the table that they refer to.**

1 I guess this guide doesn't know any funny stories.

2 Sorry, can you speak up, please?

3 Are you sure the Bayeux tapestry was made in 1400?

4 Goodness me – she's been talking for twenty minutes.

5 Did you say Monk or Munch?

	Talk 1	Talk 2	Talk 3
A Check that everyone can hear you.			
B Speak clearly and distinctly.	✓	✓	✓
C Research the subject matter.			
D Be enthusiastic and use humour.			
E Don't speak for too long.	✓	✓	✓

2))) **5.1** **Listen to three talks. Tick (✓) the things in Exercise 1 that the guides do and put a cross (✗) next to the things they don't do.**

3))) **Listen again and complete the notes.**

1 Bayeux tapestry

The tapestry was started in the ¹_____ and tells the story of the Battle of Hastings, which took place on ²_____, _____, in ³_____ vivid scenes. The tapestry is ⁴_____ long and ⁵_____ high.
Found again in ⁶_____, it has been on display since ⁷_____.

2 The Scream

Finished in ⁸_____ by Munch, *The Scream* is an ⁹_____ painting and portrays the human condition.
It was recovered in ¹⁰_____ after being stolen in February.
Dimensions: ¹¹_____ by ¹²_____

3 Family of Man

Barbara Hepworth born ¹³_____ Died 1975.
Family of man completed ¹⁴_____ . Hepworth later moved away from ¹⁵_____ and made ¹⁶_____ sculptures.

PRONUNCIATION

4))) **5.2** **Listen and choose the date in each pair that you hear.**

1 a 1725 **b** 1729

2 a 2010 **b** 2011

3 a February, 1994 **b** February, 1995

4 a November, 2012 **b** November, 2002

5 a October 14th, 1066 **b** October 14th, 1016

6 a 15th January, 1963 **b** 15th January, 1961

5))) **Listen again and practise.**

6 **Complete the sentences with the words in the box.**

abstract   bold   bronze   expressionism
light   rich

1 I love your new painting – it has a very _____ use of colours.

2 Mondrian was a great producer of _____ paintings – all colourful squares and lines.

3 _____ is the way images are used to show how people really feel.

4 The Bayeux tapestry contains deep blue and _____ red colours.

5 Gormley's statue Quantum Cloud is remarkable for the way _____ shines through it.

6 Aydin prefers carving in stone to casting in _____.

1 Read the advert and draw the route on the map.

The Sounds of Classical Germany

We invite you to explore the magical musical world of Bach, Beethoven and Wagner. During the tour you will visit some of Germany's most musical places: Dresden, Bonn and Bayreuth, as well as experiencing the delights of opera, chamber music and philharmonic concerts. Some concerts are optional so you can make your own choices about how much you hear.

WHAT'S INCLUDED IN YOUR TOUR PRICE

Airport transfer from Berlin
Private coach with English-speaking guides

Dresden:
Monday: evening concerts of Bach at Frauenkirche
Tuesday: performance at the Semper Opera (optional)

Bonn:
Wednesday: evening performance at Beethovenhalle
Thursday: Chamber music at Beethoven house
             museum (optional)

Bayreuth:
Friday: concert at Bayreuth Festspielhaus
Saturday: concert at Bayreuth Festspielhaus (optional)

PLUS ...

Accommodation, daily buffet breakfast

Dinners and lunches in Dresden, Bonn and Bayreuth

Airport transfer to Munich for return trip

2 Read the advert again and choose true (T), false (F) or no information (NI).

1 You'll be able to hear only one type of classical music. T / F / NI

2 The tour does not include all the concerts. T / F / NI

3 You can book extra nights. T / F / NI

4 All travel is by train. T / F / NI

5 The tour includes all meals. T / F / NI

3))) 5.3 Listen to a travel agent talking to the tour operator and complete the table.

Sounds of Classical Germany Itinerary

Day	Cost per concert	Travel time
Monday	€155	Berlin – Dresden _____
Tuesday	€ _____ (optional)	-
Wednesday	€176	Dresden – Bonn _____
Thursday	€ _____ (optional)	-
Friday	€250	Bonn – Bayreuth 4 hours 25 minutes
Saturday	€ _____ (optional)	-
Sunday		Bayreuth – Munich _____

Total price, including optional concerts: US $ _____

Agent's suggested price: US $ _____

4))) Listen again and answer the questions.

1 What does the tour operator say is a disadvantage of long journeys?

2 What is it about the agent's customers that makes her interested in the journey times?

3 What is the agent most concerned about?

4 How does the agent think it would be possible to reduce the cost?

5 What does the operator think the agent could lower?

6 NICHE TOURISM

UNIT MENU

Grammar: verbs followed by *-ing* and infinitive
Vocabulary: sectors in niche tourism
Professional skills: dealing with figures
Case study: improve client security

1))) **6.1** **Listen to a meeting about tourism in Equatorial Guinea. Are the statements true (T) or false (F)?**

1 Large luxury resorts make people notice the country.   T / F

2 A 'pro-poor' approach to tourism brings greater benefits to poor people.   T / F

3 Direct income is money invested in the country by the tourism company.   T / F

4 'Leakage' happens when money stays in the country.   T / F

5 Countries spend money from mass tourism on roads and facilities for the resorts.   T / F

6 A pro-poor approach is about niche tourism only.   T / F

2))) **Listen again and complete the minutes from the meeting.**

Equatorial Guinea

Advantages of mass tourism
- increases the ¹_____ of the country
- brings ²_____ expertise from multinational companies

Disadvantages of mass tourism
- about ³_____ % of income stays out of the country
- uses scarce natural ⁴_____
- people come to ⁵_____ and work in the tourist areas
- ⁶_____ causes increases in prices
- money has to be spent on ⁷_____ for the resorts

Pro-poor approach
- niche tourism develops real ⁸_____ in the community
- specialist holidays attract ⁹_____ prices
- tour operators can encourage an increase in ¹⁰_____ and give better ¹¹_____ to the hotel for local producers
- local people receive more training and are involved in making ¹²_____

3 **Complete the sentences with the words and phrases in the box.**

> benefits   growing   high spender   inflation   leakage   preference   specialized   sustainable

1 A _____ area of niche tourism is festival tourism, which has seen a big increase in numbers.

2 Avi-tourism is a very _____ part of the industry and needs people skilled in bird-watching.

3 Fran is quite rich and she's a very _____ – she always buys the best things for herself.

4 When money from tourism leaves a country, we call this _____ .

5 Prices have just gone up again! _____ must be around 10 %.

6 I have a _____ for guided tour holidays over special-interest holidays.

7 Employees at the hotel have added _____ like free access to the hotel gym.

8 Let's aim to have a more _____ way of producing power in the future and install solar panels in all our new hotels.

4 **Which answers to Exercise 3 are nouns and which are adjectives?**

5 **Answer the questions with the names of the bloggers below.**

Who writes about:

1 activities on different floors of a building? _____

2 being in a place by the sea? _____

3 going swimming? _____

Who doesn't talk about:

4 being in a hotel? _____

5 unusual health treatments? _____

6 which country or city they are in? _____

Spa Girl

Winter's coming, so Spa Girl went in search of sun and wellness. The Kamalaya Koh Samui in Thailand is a beautiful resort hotel on the coast that offers much more than a swimming pool, sauna and fitness centre. There are lots of life-changing activities to try out, like yoga, which I loved doing every morning.

Inky's blog

At Bath's thermal baths, the hot spring pools are on the ground floor, with aromatherapy steam rooms upstairs and another thermal bath on the roof, where you can sit and look out over the city! On the menu are hot stones, oriental massage and Watsu – stretching in warm water.

Brad's blog

Our hotel is built above mineral water springs so you have mineral water in the saunas and pools. There's a whole range of other things, too: I had a foot massage one day after my morning swim. Then in the afternoon, I had a chocolate massage – that's right, the masseur put chocolate on me and gave me a massage. How cool!

6 **Choose the correct verb form to complete the sentences.**

1 A friend suggested *to book / booking* into the Kamalaya Koh Samui resort hotel in Thailand.

2 Kamila didn't need *persuading / to persuade* me too much to visit her country.

3 Yesterday Diana began *feeling / to feel* poorly, so I suggested *to go / going* to the thermal baths.

4 The attendant recommended *to have / having* the hot stones treatment.

5 Jonah wanted *waiting / to wait* for his colleagues before having breakfast.

6 We really love *to be / being* here, it's so cool.

7 **Complete the sentences with the correct form of the verb in brackets.**

1 They didn't let me into the aromatherapy sauna at first, but when I called reception they admitted _____ (make) a mistake.

2 Don't forget _____ (take) your towel to the pool with you.

3 I hope you manage _____ (relax) when you're away at the Spa Hotel.

4 The tourist board plans _____ (attract) more visitors next year.

5 Try to avoid _____ (drink) the mineral water – it smells like bad eggs.

6 Come in, the manager is looking forward to _____ (meet) you.

1 Read the article and label diagrams A–C with the phrases in the box.

The Big Gig's back

It's festival time again and this year The Big Gig is bigger than ever. Over 11 days, with around 750 bands on 12 stages, the organizers are expecting more than 1.2 million people to attend – up 25% on last year. The main demographic is the 19–25-year-olds who make up 30% of the audience. Although the organizers have held ticket prices down to $170 for a week's pass,

the bad news is that the price of drinks is up 12%. However, festival organizers still expect around two out of every three people who live in the immediate area to visit the festival at some point. With such a large local attendance, the big question is whether The Big Gig is capable of attracting the all-important tourist dollar.

profile of festival goers   projected attendance increase   refreshment prices

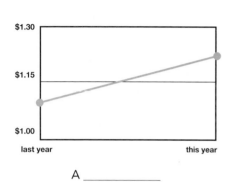

A _____

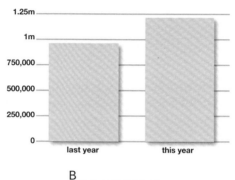

B _____

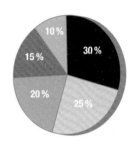

C _____

2 Read the article again and choose the correct answers.

1 There may be *1.1 / 1.3 million* people at the festival.

2 The entry fee is *the same as / higher than* last year.

3 Around *a half / two thirds* of local people will go to the festival.

4 *Most / Not much* of the money spent at the Big Gig is from local people.

PRONUNCIATION

3))) 6.2 **Listen and choose the correct figures in each pair that you hear.**

1 a 1.2million   b 1.5million

2 a $170   b $107

3 a 715   b 750

4 a 2 out of 3   b 2 out of 5

5 a 20%   b 12%

6 a ¾   b ¼

7 a 30%   b 13%

8 a 130   b ⅓

4))) **Listen again and practise.**

5))) 6.3 **Listen to a radio report about festival tourism and match the phrases 1–5 with a–e.**

1 number of festivals in the UK

2 number of 'boutique' festival goers

3 income from Isle of Wight festival (£s)

4 contribution of one festival to Scottish revenue (£s)

5 Glastonbury's annual contribution to region (£s)

a 10 million

b ¹/₇ of annual tourism income

c 7.3 million

d 200+

e between 5,000 and 35,000

6))) **Listen again and complete the programme guide.**

Tourist Talk – Nick Davies talks about festival tourism. He investigates large music festivals which attract world-famous ¹_____ stars, and the growing number of 'boutique' festivals where people go with their ²_____ and which include ³_____ and _____ as well as live concerts. Nick looks at the ⁴_____ expense of cleaning up after Glastonbury festival and the ⁵_____ in benefits to local tourism of large festivals, which recently led to the Isle of Wight being named one of the most ⁶_____ resorts in the world.

1 **Match the travel advice 1–5 with the summaries A–C. There are two more pieces of advice than you need.**

1 No restrictions in terms of travel

2 Avoid all travel to part(s) of the country

3 Avoid all travel to part(s) of the country unless it is absolutely necessary

4 Avoid all travel to the whole country

5 Avoid all travel to the whole country unless it is absolutely necessary

A We advise against all but essential travel to the eastern regions of the country. National security has still not been established and there are still occasional exchanges of fire between armed groups.

B We advise against all travel to the Republic. Our citizens should leave now while commercial transport is still available. Those who choose to remain should be aware that the Embassy will not be able to organize your evacuation. This advice to leave the country is due to continuing illegal violent protests across the country.

C Whilst most visits to the Kingdom are trouble-free, you should be aware of the increasing crime rate. You should carry some form of identification with you at all times. A photocopy of your passport is usually sufficient.

2 **Complete the travel advice with the words in the box.**

> always   avoid   don't (x2)   keep away

Essential travel to the Republic

In these times of continued political disturbance, follow the safety advice:

- Keep a low profile:
- 1 _____ wear jewellery or expensive clothes.
- 2 _____ travelling at night.
- 3 _____ go near sounds of gunfire or crowds.
- 4 _____ from armed individuals or gangs.
- 5 _____ let someone know where you are.

Register and get a reference number with smarttraveller.com so we can track your mobile phone.

3 **Find words and phrases in the texts in Exercises 1 and 2 which mean:**

1 things that are done to keep a person, building or country safe from danger or crime

2 the process of sending people away from a dangerous place to a safe place

3 not allowed by the law

4 when someone or something is safe from danger or harm

5 number that identifies a specific document or situation

4 **Complete the emails with the phrases in the box.**

> advise   appreciate   feel safe
> I can assure you
> our advice   this isn't the first incident
> understand how you feel
> worried about

From: ahmedmirza@zmail.com

To: service.consular@fo.co.uk

Dear Sir,
I was caught in a political demonstration in the main square. I'm afraid that the authorities want to arrest me. I really don't ¹ _____ now.

From: service.consular@fo.co.uk

To: ahmedmirza@zmail.com

Dear Ahmed,
Please be aware that ² _____ of this kind and that we ³ _____ in this situation. We have good communications with the authorities, so please pass your details on to the Embassy. ⁴ _____ that they will do everything they can to help.

From: mariaG@bmail.com

To: service.consular@fo.co.uk

Dear Sir,
We're ⁵ _____ travelling to the Republic but one of our relatives is seriously ill so we need to go. Could you ⁶ _____ ?

From: service.consular@fo.co.uk

To: mariaG@bmail.com

Dear Maria,
We ⁷ _____ how you feel in this situation, but ⁸ _____ is not to travel unless it is essential. Stay in contact with your family and only travel if your relative gets worse.

7 CULTURAL TOURISM

UNIT MENU

Grammar: the passive
Vocabulary: culture, linking words
Professional skills: taking part in meetings
Case study: present a proposal

1))) **7.1** **Listen to five tourists and match them with the world heritage sites a–e.**

1 _____ a a temple
2 _____ b a tomb
3 _____ c an old capital city
4 _____ d a place for growing food crops
5 _____ e a construction for defence

2))) **Listen again and choose the correct reasons the tourists visited the sites.**

1 a He planned to see the rice terraces.
  b He is bored with the beach.
2 a They learnt about a site after the trip.
  b They don't want to be like all the other tourists.
3 a She became interested in a site during a tour.
  b She was particularly interested in cultural heritage.
4 a They appreciate the significance of the site.
  b They want to visit the souvenir shop.
5 a They have relatives in the country.
  b They want to see several different sites.

3 **Match the five tourists in Exercises 1 and 2 with the cultural tourist types a–e.**

1 _____ a casual cultural tourist
2 _____ b purposeful tourist
3 _____ c sightseeing cultural tourist
4 _____ d chance discovery cultural tourist
5 _____ e incidental cultural tourist

4 **Choose the correct linking words to complete the invitation.**

SLIDE PRESENTATION – our trip to Cambodia

Dear Classmates,

We have recently returned from our fantastic trip to Cambodia and would like to invite you to a talk about it all. [1] *Although / However* we were only there for a week, we had enough time at the most important site for us, Angkor Watt, and [2] *consequently / moreover*, we were able to spend a day at another incredible site – Angkor Thom. We'll tell you about one or two unfortunate things that happened to us while we were there: our camera was stolen and [3] *as a result / on the whole*, we had to buy a new one. [4] *Consequently / Furthermore*, our hard drive crashed as we were loading the photos and [5] *consequently / although* we lost some of them. [6] *As a result / However*, we still have enough for what we hope you will think is an interesting presentation. [7] *On the whole / Consequently*, our trip was a wonderful experience and we'd like to share it with you. See you at the presentation!

5 Read the text. Are the statements true (T) or false (F)?

1 The soldiers were made for the first emperor of China.   T / F

2 8,000 figures have been found.   T / F

3 Archaeological work at the site in Shaanxi province has now finished.   T / F

4 Soldiers are the only exhibits.   T / F

5 The figures are usually on display in museums in China.   T / F

The Canadian tour of The Warrior Emperor and China's Terracotta Army opened this morning and Artscape was there to report on it.

The exhibition displays one of the most significant archaeological discoveries in history: the life-sized terracotta Chinese warriors. These extraordinary figures were created during the Qin Dynasty 2,200 years ago for Ying Zheng, who became China's first emperor after conquering the country and ending 500 years of war. He also began to create the Terracotta Army to protect him after his death.

The scale of the army is breathtaking: since 1974, approximately 2,000 warriors and horses have been found but this is only a small proportion of the total. It is estimated that there are around 8,000 of these figures and the site in China's northern Shaanxi province is still being excavated. In 1987, the site was added to the list of world heritage sites by UNESCO.

The exhibition features a wide range of sculptures – of civilians as well as military personnel – and each one is an amazing work of art on its own; seeing so many of them all together is a breathtaking experience.

The tour is significant for another reason: many of the objects on display have never before left China. In fact, some have not been displayed in any museum in the world before, not even in China. The exhibition will be taken to Montreal Museum of Fine Arts and then on to Calgary's Glenbow Museum.

6 Read the text again and find examples of the passive to complete the table.

Passive	
present simple	
present continuous	
past simple	1 _were created_ 2 _____
present perfect	1 _____ 2 _____
future	

7 Complete the sentences with the correct form of the verbs in the box.

> find   hire   produce   receive   send out   ship   update   write

1 The figures _____ to Canada last month in special crates.

2 The audio guide _____ right now and will be ready on time.

3 Audio guides to the exhibition can _____ for just $10 per visit.

4 The exhibition is great for children – interactive displays about the history of the army _____ by museum staff at the moment.

5 When the exhibition opens, visitors _____ a special Terracotta Army badge.

6 Since 1974, over 2,000 soldiers _____ by archaeologists.

7 The website _____ several times since it went live last month.

8 Press releases _____ to local and international media next week.

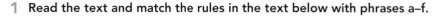

1 **Read the text and match the rules in the text below with phrases a–f.**

a by checking that everyone agrees before moving on to the next point

b because finding the best solutions is the purpose of the meeting

c not blaming individuals

d so that there are no distractions

e and give them all your full attention

f because everyone needs to be clear about the objectives

Running an effective meeting

A good meeting can be very useful – employees can learn directly about new policies or participate in decisions affecting them. Meetings can be held to pass on or gather information, solve problems or make decisions.

Here are some rules to include:

- State the purpose at the start of the meeting, [1]____

- Don't allow interruptions so that everyone can contribute.

- Try to understand the pros and cons of all suggestions [2]____

A bad meeting, on the other hand, can be a waste of time. Having a purpose, good preparation, setting an agenda and having clear guidelines can turn a bad meeting into an effective meeting, and discussion guidelines can help make a meeting run smoothly.

- There should be no private conversations during the meeting.

- Participants should keep to the subject under discussion [3]____

- Keep the meeting together, [4]____

- Discussion should be about understanding the problem, [5]____

- Listen to participants [6]____

---

2))) **7.2** **Listen to a meeting and decide if it is a good or bad meeting.**

3))) **Listen again and decide which rules in activity 1 they break.**

4))) **7.3** **Listen to another meeting and say what two agenda items they discuss.**

5))) **Listen again and complete the notes from the second meeting.**

Marketing meeting notes

Fringe festival attracts [1]_____ people: organizers want to increase to [2]_____ .

Organizers to expand team by [3]_____ and increase number of events to [4]_____ .

Their budget is [5]_____ , of which [6]_____ will be spent on advertising, with [7]_____ fliers sent by post.

Need to plan to market for [8]_____ people.

---

6 **Complete the sentences from the second meeting.**

1 We're _____ about the marketing for the festival.

2 _____ begin?

3 The first _____ is the size of the festival.

4 Silvia, do you have _____ ?

5 Do _____ we're all in agreement with Gunther?

6 Can we _____ the next item, then?

7 I think _____ everything.

7))) **Listen to the second meeting again and check your answers.**

PRONUNCIATION

8))) **7.4** **Listen to the closed questions and practise the fall-rise intonation.**

1 Do you have anything to say?

2 Shall we begin?

3 Do you have anything to add?

4 Can we move on to the next item, then?

5 Is there any other business?

1 **Read the texts below and choose the correct words to complete the sentences.**

1 Doha's *oil / heritage* helped it win the City of Culture award.

2 Doha has two very different *characteristics / attractions*.

3 Before 1990, Glasgow had a poor *tourist industry / image*.

4 Glasgow is now *City of Culture / a great tourist destination*.

5 The population of São Luis is made up of people from *one culture/many cultures*.

Undoubtedly, the discovery of oil started Doha's phenomenal growth into a modern city. But its long traditions, cultural heritage and modern skyline helped it win the 2010 nomination for City of Culture and raise its international profile.

Glasgow was a significant choice for City of Culture in 1990. Glasgow's reputation was bad and its economy was worse but cultural tourism gave a new dynamic to the city and enhanced the city's image in the eyes of Glaswegians. Glasgow was the first city in Europe to use cultural tourism to regenerate the city and is now one of the world's must-see cities.

São Luis, Brazil, is a charming place with a diverse multicultural population that gives the city its unique cultural richness. São Luis city centre is an enchanting place of winding streets and colonial houses. By becoming the Americas' Capital of Culture, São Luis was able to preserve its heritage sites.

2 **Tick (✓) the benefits of becoming a City of Culture, according to the texts.**

1 better choice of visitor attractions _____

2 rebuilding the city _____

3 citizens have more pride in the city _____

4 increased money from tourism _____

5 incentive to keep historical places _____

6 an increased profile internationally _____

3 **Read the proposal and match the headings below with paragraphs 1–4.**

> Economic benefits   Executive summary
> Methodology   Programme description

1 _____
Newcastle has made a unique contribution to popular culture. This proposal promotes Newcastle as European City of Culture as part of a sustainable tourism strategy to regenerate the city through the economic benefits cultural tourism brings.

2 _____
Newcastle has great potential for exploiting its rich and diverse cultural history. The themes for the programme are: create, integrate and regenerate.

3 _____
• Focus groups will be held to generate ideas for events throughout the City of Culture year.
• Organizations with a good track record of managing large events like the Great North Run will be invited to participate
• Regeneration plans for old industrial sites along the river and disused docks will be drawn up to include new museums and art galleries.

4 _____
The financial advantages of cultural tourism are potentially enormous. If Newcastle becomes City of Culture, we estimate that approximately 3.5 million new visitors will come to the city, bringing £800 million of income. In addition, new buildings such as a new opera house and shipbuilding museum will have a lasting effect.

4 **Read the proposal again. Which paragraphs include the following points? There are two points which are not in the proposal.**

City of Culture shortlist

The proposal needs to:
• have a solid organizational structure _____
• highlight cultural diversity _____
• include the events in the programme _____
• show sustainable and long-term regeneration and development _____
• have a budget from different national and private sources _____
• include participation of citizens _____
• present the programme's main subject areas _____

8 RUNNING A HOTEL

8

UNIT MENU

Grammar: *have/get* something done
Vocabulary: *-ed/-ing* adjectives, word combinations
Professional skills: making presentations
Case study: Transform the team

---

1 Read the advert and answer the questions.

1 What is the main role of the assistant manager?

2 Which three departments involved with guests will they manage?

3 What are the other two main responsibilities?

Assistant Hotel Manager
Galway, Ireland

Job type: Permanent, full time

Salary: €26,000 – accommodation included

The Howatt Hotel is seeking an enthusiastic assistant manager.

Are you energetic enough to help manage a five-star hotel?

Duties involve working weekends and evenings, managing front-of-house departments such as reception, conferencing and refreshment areas. You need to be hard-headed in a fast-moving business environment, good with figures and trustworthy when dealing with large amounts of money.

A major part of the role is customer relations and you need to be outgoing and friendly – even with the most demanding guests. If you meet these requirements, please contact HR at personnel@howatthotel.com.

2 Read the advert again and find words which mean:

1 feeling or showing a lot of interest and excitement about something _____

2 able to work a lot without feeling tired _____

3 practical and able to make difficult decisions without letting your emotions affect your judgment _____

4 dependable and honest _____

5 interested in meeting and talking to new people _____

3 Choose the correct alternatives in the conversation.

A How are things going today?

B Well, I'm feeling very ¹*tiring / tired* – it's not been a very ²*rewarding / rewarded* day.

A Why? What happened?

B I spent all day hanging around for a delivery. It was really ³*boring / bored*. Chef placed an order with our food supplier for today but it didn't come.

A Really?

B Yes, I was a bit ⁴*surprising / surprised* – the food suppliers are usually very good. I guess they couldn't get the jackfruit Chef wanted in Scotland.

A And what did Chef say?

B Well, she was very ⁵*irritating / irritated* about it, which I could understand. I suggested making something else.

A Good idea.

B But she wasn't ⁶*interesting / interested* in my opinion. So she tried some different suppliers … and told me to wait here for their delivery! I hope they turn up soon.

A No, you really aren't having a good day, are you?

4 Choose the correct multi-word verb to complete the sentences.

1 Peter, can we meet later? I've got a hundred things to *run out of / get through* before lunch.

2 Quickly, get the bellhops – the 7 o'clock group has *turned up / seen to* early.

3 Wendy is really upset. She's just *talked about / found out* she's on night shift.

4 Could you get me some more notepaper? We've *caught up on / run out of* it.

5 We need to order a taxi to *pick up / put up* some new guests from the airport.

5 Match the problems 1–5 with the requests a–e.

1 She's lost. _e_
2 They're very heavy. __
3 We've run out. __
4 They're filthy. __
5 It's broken. __

a Please get the windows cleaned.
b Get more menus printed.
c Have that mirror replaced, please.
d Have the porter take the cases to room 101.
e Get the porter to show her where her room is.

6 Read the emails to the maintenance manager from the hotel staff. Complete them with *get/have* + the correct form of the verb in brackets

| A | 9.40 pm | from | Simon McKinzey, restaurant manager | subject | chairs in restaurant |

Mike, there are three ripped chairs in the restaurant. Could you _____ the porter _____ them next week? (replace)

| B | 7.30 am | from | Paula Braschi, kitchen worker | subject | dishwasher |

Mike, the dishwasher's not working. Can you _____ it _____ ? Call the service engineer today. (repair)

| C | 12.40 pm | from | Donna Carole, housekeeper | subject | paint behind the pictures |

When you take the picture down in room 44, please _____ the decorator _____ the wall. (repaint)

| D | 14.40 pm | from | Joanna Macmillan, manager | subject | urgent repairs |

Dear Mike, The report from the safety inspection isn't very good. The electrics in the kitchen are terrible. We need to _____ the whole kitchen _____ . (rewire) Can you get the electrician in?

7 Read the customer satisfaction sheet and complete 1–5 with these words.

> acknowledged   appearance   assistance   choice   promptness

Area: Restaurant Juice Bar		Score this year	% improvement
Items checked	Report (last year)		
A Greeting guests	Guests were not greeted or [1]_____; the waitress wasn't very friendly at all.	40	____%
B Help with menu selection	When the waitress finally noticed me, I asked for [2]_____ as there were several fruit juices I didn't know. Unfortunately, the waitress didn't know them either.	____	0 %
C Availability of drinks	I made my [3]_____ and asked for the most difficult drink on the menu and surprisingly the Juice Bar had it.	____	0 %
D Speed of service	The [4]_____ of the service was surprisingly quick.	____	____%
E Staff dress	The [5]_____ of the waitress was good; she was tidy and smart	____	____
Total score and rating for all 5 items	50 (= very poor); 100 (= poor);150 (= average); 200 (= good); 250 (= excellent)	____ (= good)	average total ____%

8))) 8.1 Listen to this year's report. Complete the scores and show the average percentage improvement.

1 Look at the advice on presentations. Tick (✓) the things you should do and put a cross (✗) next to the things you shouldn't do.

1 ____ move around a lot

2 ____ think about the audience

3 ____ stick to the plan

4 ____ rehearse the presentation

5 ____ turn your back to the audience

6 ____ put a lot of text on your slides

7 ____ have a clear structure

8 ____ forget to have copies of your slides

Slide A __

End of the presentation
- Don't be impolite, even with silly questions.

Slide B __

During (2)
- Don't put too much text on the slides.
- Never read from the slides – keep good eye contact.

Slide C __

During (1)
- Always greet the audience at the start.
- Don't digress – stick to your plan.
- Guide your audience through the presentation with a clear structure.

Slide D __

Effective presentations
Sue Dawson
- How do you feel before a presentation?
- What's a presentation for?

2 Sue Dawson is going to give a presentation. Look at her slides and put them in the order in which she will use them.

3))) 8.2 Listen and check your answers.

4))) Listen again and complete the notes from the presentation.

Definition: a presentation is to ¹_____ , pass on information or teach something.

It's important to think about ²_____ and to practise and ³_____ as much as possible.

Say hello and say who you are and which ⁴_____ you are from.

Keep your audience ⁵_____ by telling them what they want to know.

Tell them what you're going to tell them. Then ⁶_____ them. Finally, tell your audience what you ⁷_____. Deal with questions ⁸_____ and clearly.

Slide E __

Three parts to a presentation:
1 before   2 during   3 after
Before
a) What's the most important thing to think about?
b) How to feel confident?

PRONUNCIATION

5 Put the words into the correct group according to their stress pattern.

confident effective finally impression
information interesting preparation
presentation presenter

A ● • •   1 _confident_
            2 _____
            3 _____

B • ● •   1 _____
            2 _____
            3 _____

C • • ● •   1 _____
            2 _____
            3 _____

6))) 8.3 Listen and check. Then listen and practise.

1 Read the recommendations section from a consultancy company's report on the Howatt Hotel and tick (✓) the problems it mentions.

1 delays ____   **5** too little training ____

2 old technology ____   **6** bad communications ____

3 little flexibility ____   **7** too much direct management ____

4 poor leadership ____   **8** high staffing levels ____

Recommendations

After reviewing the hotel's service score (10 out of 100), this report found major problems in three key areas.

1 Central management decision-making leads to poor flexibility and low job satisfaction.

2 Direct management in daily operations causes inefficiency and poor staff morale. At the moment, managers are heavily involved in daily interaction with guests and directing front-of-house operations.

3 Poor communications due to 1 and 2 above lead to low productivity in hotel services and poor customer satisfaction ratings.

The report makes the following recommendations.

1 Team leaders should be created and given responsibility for operational decision-making. At the moment when employees need something or want to deal with a problem, they have to wait for a decision from their manager. This results in poor flexibility, delays and inefficiency.

2 Less direct management: the focus of the managers should not be daily interaction with the guests. Managers should not take direct responsibility for every job in the hotel. Interfering with daily work reduces staff morale.

3 More training: if the hotel managers give more decision-making to team leaders, then the team leaders need training. Training staff makes the hotel more efficient and gives the staff greater job satisfaction. It also leads to a better guest experience and repeat customer stays.

2 Read the report again and find words which mean:

1 the ability to change or be changed easily _____

2 the happiness you feel when you succeed or get what you want from your work _____

3 the confidence and hope that a person or group feels _____

4 getting involved in a situation where you are not wanted _____

5 working well, without wasting time or energy _____

3))) 8.4 Listen to the management consultant's post-report interviews. Tick (✓) the recommendations 1–3 from the report in Exercise 1 that the staff talk about.

Interviewee	Recommendation		
1 Mr Roche	1_____	2_____	3_____
2 Mrs Gonzalez	1_____	2_____	3_____
3 Ms Yeboah	1_____	2_____	3_____

4))) Listen again and choose what happened after the report.

Recommendation 1

a the manager still makes all the decisions

b individual staff take important decisions

c team leaders take decisions

Recommendation 2

a the manager stays in his office

b the manager still interferes

c the manager never interferes

Recommendation 3

a staff have no training

b staff have some training

c staff have a training programme

5 Answer the questions.

1 Which was the most popular recommendation?

2 Which was the most effective recommendation?

UNIT MENU

Grammar: question forms
Vocabulary: customer service terms, personal qualities
Professional skills: handling telephone conversations
Case study: improve customer service

1 Read the thread and decide what the common problem was. Choose the correct option.

a not being able to solve a problem

b cultural differences in customer relations

c being impolite

d aggressive customers

Customer service forum

Thread: What did I get wrong?

21:44 latest comment

Toshi, Japan

You're all lucky. I actually lost my job for smiling too much at a woman from Peru, who was at one of my tables in the restaurant. She thought I was being too personal and that I don't care about my work, which is not the case.

21:15

Julia, UK

Well, last week a couple from the Middle East reported a stolen passport. I wanted to sort it out quickly so, rather than show I cared, I got down to business immediately. I was trying to be efficient and competent but the couple's feedback form said my behaviour wasn't appropriate because I was too impersonal.

16:27

Ahmed, Rihad

You can't win sometimes! I was in a meeting the other day with two Europeans when my mobile phone rang. Naturally, I interrupted the meeting to answer the phone – in my culture it's impolite not to – but the other people couldn't believe it. They thought it was disrespectful!

11.00

Tracey, New York

See what happened to me the other day – I was at the hotel reception trying to be really friendly when a customer from Holland came to the desk. He asked me lots of questions and I was very polite saying please and thank you after each sentence. I thought I was being welcoming but the customer didn't – he complained to my boss saying I was pretending to be nice.

2 Read the thread again. Are the statements true (T) or false (F)?

1 Toshi isn't serious about his job. T /F

2 Julia's main aim was to find a solution to the problem. T /F

3 Julia wasn't worried about how they felt. T /F

4 Europeans normally answer a mobile phone in a meeting. T /F

5 Tracey wasn't attempting to be polite. T /F

6 The customer thought Tracey was not behaving in a sincere way. T /F

3 Find 12 negative adjectives in the wordsquare. All the adjectives are related to personal qualities and some are in the thread in Exercise 1.

N	F	I	Z	G	Y	I	U	B	D	E	I	H	X	F	U	I	D
Z	B	N	D	I	S	L	O	Y	A	L	C	Y	E	A	X	I	U
U	I	E	K	N	G	X	R	Z	I	A	X	I	R	N	E	N	N
N	N	F	P	B	T	K	E	G	N	Q	D	Y	R	P	I	S	W
A	C	F	M	Z	Z	O	X	B	A	E	I	B	K	W	Y	J	E
N	O	I	G	U	X	R	W	B	P	X	W	D	U	M	R	F	L
P	M	C	D	I	S	R	E	S	P	E	C	T	F	U	L	F	C
W	P	I	F	C	Z	R	S	C	R	Q	E	T	W	U	N	D	O
A	E	E	D	O	R	U	K	I	O	J	B	T	I	N	B	I	M
F	T	N	B	M	O	S	H	D	P	L	Y	D	G	R	Z	S	I
L	E	T	O	H	F	T	H	Q	R	B	N	Y	M	E	U	H	N
D	N	Y	T	I	M	P	A	T	I	E	N	T	C	L	E	O	G
E	T	N	L	C	F	N	A	F	A	W	F	Z	I	I	B	N	W
I	M	P	O	L	I	T	E	R	T	C	Y	N	Y	A	Y	E	M
P	E	W	J	C	K	M	I	L	E	H	I	L	D	B	D	S	C
V	J	U	N	F	R	I	E	N	D	L	Y	G	P	L	B	T	T
Z	N	Z	I	M	P	E	R	S	O	N	A	L	O	E	O	U	I

4 Put the questions in the survey in the correct order.

Travelogue customer satisfaction survey

Name: Barry Adams

Email: bazza@apl.com

1 you you me where went could tell?
_____

2 you did holiday enjoy your?
_____

Yes ☐   Not really ☐   No ☐

3 your idea where you get the did for holiday?
_____

TV ☐   Radio ☐   Internet ☐
Friends ☐   Other ☐

4 what special about the was holiday?
_____

Exotic location ☐
Learning new things ☐
Cultural experience ☐
Meeting new people ☐

5 tell holiday could you where you me bought your?
_____

Online ☐   National travel company ☐
Small travel agent ☐

6 products around shop you for did similar?
_____

Yes ☐   No ☐

7 holiday do the you think good value was?
_____

Yes ☐   Not really ☐   No ☐

8 you could me rate holiday how your tell you would?
_____

1 ☐
2 ☐
3 ☐
4 ☐
5 ☐   (1=poor, 5=excellent)

5))) 9.1 Listen and tick (✓) the answers Barry gives to complete the questionnaire.

6))) Listen again and complete the notes.

Customer went to Italy to learn about italian
¹ _____.

Found out about it through an advert during a TV
² _____ _____.

Bought holiday at a ³ _____ travel agent.

Note: thinks ⁴ _____ to someone
⁵ _____ is v. important.

Didn't look at the ⁶ _____ as their prices wouldn't affect choice.

Got a ⁷ _____ % discount for ⁸ _____ the holiday in advance.

7 Correct the mistakes in the questions.

1 Are you have a few moments to answer a brief questionnaire?
2 Would I take your name?
3 Do you mind if I taking your email address?
4 You go to the travel agent to book it?
5 Do you know who can I ask for help with this?
6 Can I asking if you looked at the competition?
7 Would you mind telling me if did you get a discount?
8 Would you considering buying a holiday from the same travel agent?

8 Complete the sentences with the phrases in the box. There is one more phrase than you need.

can I ask you   can I see   could you possibly
could you tell   do you know whether
have you any idea   would you mind

1 Hello, my name's Stefan from Travelogue customer services. _____ answering a few questions?
2 I know all flights are delayed but _____ of the arrival time?
3 _____ take over at reception while I show Mrs Blunt to her room?
4 _____ me what time the show begins? I hope we're not too late to get in.
5 _____ Mr Toda booked a room with a twin or a double bed?
6 Our bar facilities are only for people over the age of 18. _____ your identification?

1)))) **9.2** **Listen to four conversations and complete the messages.**

A

From: *Eddie*

To: *Rita*

Eddie is going to be [1] _____ ; *you can call him on* [2] _____ .

B

Room booking request from Hans Gert on 4922 [3] _____ .

C

INCIDENT REPORT FORM

Customer name: Erica Wong

Problem: left [4] _____ in taxi

Time: [5] _____

From: Central station to [6] _____

Contact number: [7] _____

Email: [8] _____ @qmail.com

D

Video chat names:

Frank = [9] _____

Angie = [10] _____

2)))) **Listen again and choose the correct options to complete the sentences.**

1 The reason Eddie is late is because
  a there are lots of cars on the road
  b he's bringing brochures to the office

2 Hans wanted to speak to
  a the hotel restaurant
  b the hotel reception

3 Erica travelled to Seattle by
  a train
  b taxi

4 The people arrange to call each other later
  a by phone
  b on a computer

3 **Complete the sentences from the telephone conversations with the phrases in the box.**

come through   cut off   get back
hold on   I'm on   pass on
put you through   read that back   ring off
running out   sort it out   topped it up

1 Your call is very important to us, so please leave a message and we'll _____ to you as soon as possible.

2 Hi, it's Eddie – can you _____ a message to Rita?

3 I'm sorry, sir, you've _____ to the wrong department.

4 _____ a moment and I'll _____ to room bookings.

5 Just in case we're _____ , let me take your number.

6 Let me _____ to you – 49 – that's Germany, isn't it? – 221 7897650.

7 _____ Seattle 33 95 874.

8 OK, madam, leave it with us. I'll _____ for you and get back to you later today.

9 My phone's _____ of money – I'll call you back after I've _____ .

10 Don't ring me back – just _____ now and go on video chat.

4 **Match the possible responses with five of the sentences in Exercise 3.**

a Thank you so much, and I look forward to hearing from you. _____

b Yes, of course. Have you got a pen? _____

c Sorry? Could you tell me again what your number is? _____

d No, it's probably easier if I call you. Is your battery OK? _____

e Oh, sorry, I obviously didn't press the right number. _____

PRONUNCIATION

5)))) **9.3** **Listen and choose the number or name and number in each pair that you hear.**

1 **a** 0444 482 9635   **b** 0444 482 5635

2 **a** 36 1 336851   **b** 36 1 3368511

3 **a** 00 44 141 3336699   **b** 00 44 141 3336655

4 **a** W.Stanley@zmail.com   **b** w.stanley@zmail.com

5 **a** LiPeng50   **b** LiPeng15

6)))) **Listen again and practise.**

1 Put the letter of complaint in the correct order.

1 ____ 2 ____ 3 ____ 4 ____ 5 ____

Dear Sir,

A We would like full compensation for the holiday of £300, plus £125 spent on travel. Please contact me at erikrolinsak@qmail.co.uk. I look forward to settling this at the earliest possible time.

B We believed that we would have a relaxing weekend at Glen Douglas but were not told in advance that the hotel was in the middle of extensive renovations. The noise from the building work started early so we were woken up both mornings. If we had been told in advance, we could have booked another hotel.

C As a consequence of the very poor standards we experienced in August at the Glen Douglas Country Hotel, it is with regret that I am writing to you to make a complaint.

D More importantly, due to the building work, the air in the hotel was full of dust. This caused a lot of problems for my wife, who has breathing difficulties.

E Finally, many facilities were not available, for example, the swimming pool was closed and there was no sauna.

Yours faithfully,

Erik Rolinska

2 Read the letter again and answer the questions. Choose the correct options.

1 What is Erik's most serious complaint?

  a noise

  b lack of facilities

  c poor air quality

2 The building work at the hotel was

  a limited

  b widespread

  c not noticeable.

3 What did Erik say he would have liked to receive before booking?

  a an early-booking discount

  b a letter about what was happening

  c a brochure for a different hotel

4 What solution does Erik suggest?

  a a part refund

  b a complete refund

  c a complete refund plus expenses

3 Complete the manager's reply with the phrases in the box.

> attempted to warn   due to
> gesture of goodwill   no alternative
> prepared to offer   regret that

Dear Mr Rolinska,

A We ¹ _____ you were dissatisfied with the service at Glen Douglas Country Hotel. Our guests usually return from their stay at the hotel satisfied with their experience but ² _____ essential renovation work, our normal excellent standards were not met.

B We ³ _____ all our guests about the work but it seems you did not receive our letter.

C In order to refurbish the hotel, we had to close some parts of the building. We attempted to do building work when guests would be least disturbed. However, at times we had ⁴ _____ other than to go ahead with the work.

D As a ⁵ _____ we are ⁶ _____ you a refund of £300, i.e. the cost of your stay.

4 Read the reply again and match 1–4 with paragraphs A–D.

1 state what action was taken ____

2 provide an explanation ____

3 make an offer ____

4 apologize for the unpleasant experience ____

10 BUSINESS TRAVEL

UNIT MENU

Grammar: past perfect
Vocabulary: idioms and metaphors
Professional skills: socializing and making small talk
Case study: at a Trade Fair

1 Read the text. Are the statements true (T) or false (F)?

1 Although a company's financial situation may not be good, business travel is a good investment.   T / F

2 Business travel takes up time that could be spent on more important tasks.   T / F

3 Travelling on business has less of an impact on personal relationships than on work.   T / F

4 Half of all business trips are undertaken by manufacturing companies.   T / F

5 The quality of virtual meetings needs to be improved.   T / F

2 Read the text again and complete the chart.

3 Find phrases in the text which mean:

1 cut to the bone _____

2 going through the roof _____

3 putting the brakes on _____

4 on a shoestring _____

5 foots the bill _____

6 on the horizon _____

Bad business travel

The romantic idea of the business executive flying to distant countries is very appealing. In fact, business travel is seen as essential even when budgets are being reduced to a minimum: to seek new partners, win new contracts and maintain business relationships. However, there are disadvantages to consider.

On average, medium-sized businesses can spend 10% of their overall budget on business travel, and with costs increasing at an alarming rate, this represents a significant amount. Although it's possible to work while travelling, it's difficult to be fully available for colleagues. Moreover, due to the complexity of itineraries, meetings tend to take longer than they need to, thus reducing the speed of other work that is more urgent.

Business travel can be stressful, too. A survey for Microsoft showed that nearly three quarters of respondents found business trips more stressful than going to the dentist. One fifth said business trips had a negative affect on work and 40% reported negative effects on their family. There's a clear link between poor health and business trips, which often cause lack of sleep, unhealthy diets (obesity is 92% more common in business travellers) and unusual levels of stress. Jet lag causes tiredness and loss of memory but even though it takes time to recover from a long journey, business travellers can't afford rest days when they're doing everything for as little money as possible.

Finally, it's the environment that also has to pay for business travel – half of carbon emissions in non-manufacturing industry are caused by work-related travel. With the threat of global warming in the near future, we have to look forward to the day when virtual meetings are of good enough quality to reduce business travel significantly.

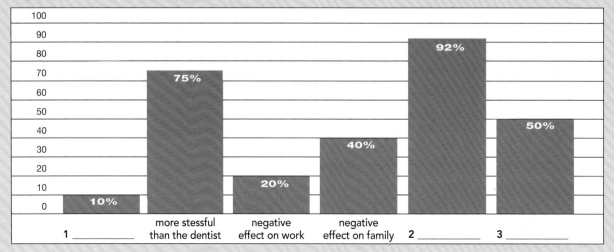

4 Read the advert and tick (✓) the activities it mentions.

 1 ___

 2 ___

 3 ___

 4 ___

 5 ___

> 'I thought I'd tried every method to get my staff working as a team – then I found Incentivize.'
>
> **Dave, Peterborough**
>
> 'We'd searched all over for a company to lead team-building days. Fortunately, Incentivize found us.'
>
> **Maryam, London**
>
> Are you looking for ways to energize and build your team? We offer exciting team-building away days, including paintballing, bungee-jumping and whitewater rafting.
>
> **Let us contact you – send your email address now to Dawson.Linda@ incentivize.com**

5 Read the advert again and choose the correct answers.

1 What was Dave's problem?
  a His staff didn't work well together.
  b His staff weren't motivated.

2 What was Maryam's problem?
  a Her staff didn't like team-building days.
  b A team-building company was hard to find.

6))) **10.1** Listen and say which activity in Exercise 1 the speaker talks about. Was it a good experience?

7))) Listen again and put the events in the order they happened.

_____ They started paintballing.

_____ Paintballing was chosen.

_____ They wrote a letter of complaint.

_____ They divided into two teams.

_____ They arrived back at the office.

_____ Verity organized an away day.

__1__ An advert came through the post.

_____ The guns stopped working.

_____ An old bus picked them up.

8))) **10.2** Listen and complete the sentences with past simple or past perfect verbs.

1 Two days before that, an advert _____ to the office for Incentivize.

2 Their instructor _____ her health and safety test.

3 Early that morning, an old bus _____ us up at the office.

4 Unfortunately, it _____ five kilometres before the paintball area.

5 By 1:20 the paintball guns _____ working.

6 So we _____ to go back to the office.

7 Our team _____ a long letter of complaint.

8 So I guess the teamwork activity _____!

9 Complete the story with the past simple or past perfect of the verbs in brackets.

> Last week our boss [1]_____ (organize) a staff party at a posh restaurant in the centre of town. Earlier that week, she [2]_____ (speak) to the restaurant owner. He said that we could go any time because the restaurant [3]_____ (be) quiet all the previous week. So my boss [4]_____ (book) the restaurant and told all of us that the company would pay for the meal – we [5]_____ (win) a major contract the week before and she wanted to celebrate. When the day of the party arrived, we [6]_____ (leave) the office early and headed for the city centre. What a disappointment when we got there – the restaurant [7]_____ (shut down) due to lack of business, but they [8]_____ (not tell) our boss and we were left outside with nowhere to go.

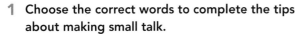
1 Choose the correct words to complete the tips about making small talk.

1 Make a *nice / rude* remark about where you are and what's happening.

2 Ask *open / closed* questions.

3 *Never / Try to* make personal remarks about the other person, e.g. their clothes, hair, etc.

4 Have something interesting to say; it's best *to talk / not to talk* about politics or religion.

5 Be careful about your personal space – *stand as close as possible to / keep a distance from* the other person.

6 Have an exit line ready so that you can end the conversation *abruptly / politely*.

2))) **10.3** Listen to four conversations A–D and say which tips in Exercise 1 were not followed.

3 Complete the conversation with open questions.

J: Luke, long time, no see.

L: Hi, Justin.

J: ¹_____?

L: I've been here for about ten minutes.

J: Right. ²_____?

L: I arrived early this morning.

J: ³_____ ?

L: Oh, fine, thanks. It was a very good journey.

J: ⁴_____?

L: Work is going quite well at the moment, thanks.

J: Good. ⁵_____?

L: The family are all well, thank you.

4 Read the conversation endings and complete the gaps with the phrases in the box.

> afraid I have to go   catch up
> excuse me for a minute
> I must dash   see you   take care

1 A: Oh, Richard, look at the time – _____ .

B: OK – good to see you again.

2 A: Well, I'm _____ . I've got an early start tomorrow and I need to get some sleep.

B: Yes, me too – _____ tomorrow, then, first thing.

3 A: Can you _____? I must say hello to Francine over there – she's one of our most important clients.

B: Go ahead – we'll _____ later.

4 Lovely to see you again, Andy. See you at the next conference and in the meantime, _____ .

PRONUNCIATION

5))) **10.4** Listen to the tag questions below and do the following.

1 Mark the questions ↗ if the intonation rises at the end and ↘ if it falls at the end.

2 Write I if the speaker is asking for information and C if the speaker is asking for confirmation.

1 You're Neil, aren't you? _____

2 It's been a long day, hasn't it? _____

3 The brochures were here, weren't they? _____

4 Professor Yang, isn't it? _____

5 The trip is on Sunday, isn't it? _____

6 I didn't expect to see Mary here, did you? _____

7 It's not eight o'clock already, is it? _____

8 The food's superb, isn't it? _____

6))) Listen again and practise.

1))) **10.5** Listen and match conversation extracts A–F with some of the squares in the Trade Fair Game.

START

1 Check in at your hotel.

2 Talk about the journey.

3 Talk about the weather.

4 Ask another delegate about themselves.

5 You're late for your next appointment. Phone for a taxi.

12 A visitor comes to your stand to talk about shared business interests.

FINISH

6 Say goodbye to someone politely.

11 A delegate asks you what you think about major tourist events in your country.

10 You meet someone who was on the same course as you. Talk about the course and what you learnt.

9 At the restaurant, ask a delegate about the food.

8 A delegate asks you to recommend a good restaurant.

7 Invite a delegate for a meal.

2))) Listen again and complete the extracts.

A F = Francois   P = Piera

F: Look, Piera, I've really enjoyed talking to you but _____ now to the seminar on Virtual Marketing.

P: Well, _____ meet up later to continue our conversation?

B R = Receptionist   P = Piera

R: Hello, madam. _____ your name?

P: Hi. I'm Piera Chow. _____ for three nights.

R: Just a moment, Ms Chow. I'll just _____.

C P = Piera   F = Francois

P: Yes, _____ hotpot is a Sichuan _____ . Do you like it?

F: It's _____ .

D F = Francois   P = Piera

F: I was going to call room service and eat in my room.

P: I've got a better idea. _____ going out for dinner together?

E P = Piera   T = Tom

P: I see. My name's Piera Chow. Here's _____ .

T: I'm Tom Gross. Here's my card. We've seen good growth in our _____ branch of the business.

P: Yes, we're quite _____ – it's an idea that's just come to our country.

F P = Piera   R = Receptionist

P: It feels quite _____ today.

R: Yes, I'm afraid it hasn't been very good this week. It's been _____ and _____ .

3 Match the words and phrases to make collocations.

1 conference _____   a outlook
2 niche _____   b loyalty programme
3 economic _____   c delegate
4 hotel guest _____   d tourism
5 customer _____   e service

4 Complete the sentences with the phrases in Exercise 3.

1 Business is picking up – and the latest forecast says that the _____ is good.

2 Festival tourism is a small but growing area of the market – it's a good example of _____ .

3 Madam, before you check out, could I interest you in our _____ so that you can stay at a better rate next time you come?

4 There were over 1,000 _____ at our Travel Expo in Doha last year.

5 I'm sorry you didn't like the room. I'll put you through to our _____ team so that they can deal with your complaint.

TOURISM TERMS

People

ADL	Adult
CHD	Child
INF	Infant (up to two years old)
MR	Mister
MISS	Used before a single woman's family name
MRS	Used before a married woman's family name
MS	Used before a woman's family name when she does not want to be called 'Mrs' or 'Miss'
PAX	Passengers
VIP	Very important person
VFR	Visiting Friends and Relatives

International organizations

ATLAS	The Association for Tourism and Leisure Education
ETC	European Travel Commission
EU	European Union
IATA	International Air Transport Association – industry trade group for airlines which regulates international air travel
ICAO	International Civil Aviation Organization
IOC	International Olympic Committee
ISO	International Organization for Standardization
NTO	National Tourism Organization (organization a government uses to promote the country)
TIC	Tourist Information Centre
UN	United Nations
UNESCO	United Nations Educational, Scientific and Cultural Organization
VIC	Visitor Information Centre
WTO	World Tourism Organization (also UNWTO)
WHS	World Heritage Site

Jobs in tourism

ASST	Assistant
CEO	Chief Executive Officer
CFO	Chief Financial Officer
CV	Curriculum vitae
DOB	Date of birth
EHK	Executive Housekeeper
FOM	Front Office Manager
FT	Full-time
GM	General Manager
HK	Housekeeper
HQ	Headquarters
HR	Human Resources
HRS	Hours of work
MOD	Manager on duty
PERM	Permanent position
PT	Part-time
TA	Travel agent
TEMP	Temporary position
P/H	Rate of pay per hour
P/W	Per week
P.A.	Per annum (annual salary)

Times and time zones

a.m.	from midnight to noon
p.m.	after noon

12-hour clock	24-hour clock
12:10 a.m.	0010
03:05 a.m.	0305
07.59 p.m.	1959

The 24-hour clock is simpler than the 12-hour clock. It uses four continuous digits (from 0000 to 2400) and there is no a.m. or p.m.

CST	Central Standard Time
EST	Eastern Standard Time
GMT	Greenwich Mean Time
PST	Pacific Standard Time
UTC	Coordinated Universal Time
WST	Western Standard Time

24/7	24 hours a day, 7 days a week
HRS	Hours
WKS	Weeks

Money and prices

Add-ons	Additional tour features that are not included in tour price
Approx	Approximately
ATM	Automatic Teller Machine (Am Eng), Cash machine (Br Eng)
B	Billions
EXCL	Exclusive (not everything is included in the price)
FIT	Fully inclusive tour
GDP	Gross Domestic Product
GIT	Group Inclusive Tour
GST	General Sales Tax (Am Eng)
IBAN	International Bank Account Number
IIT	Individual Inclusive Tour
INCL	Inclusive
IT	Inclusive tour
K	Thousands
M	Millions
PIN	Personal Identification Number
POS	Point-of-sales terminal (small hand-held computer for servers to take orders and calculate bills)
PP	Per person
VAT	Value added tax (Br Eng)

ISO Currency codes

*World's top ten most traded currencies

AUD	Australian Dollar*
CAD	Canadian Dollar*
CNY	Chinese Yuan Renminbi
EUR	Euro*
GBP	United Kingdom Pound*
HKD	Hong Kong Dollar*
INR	Indian Rupee
JPY	Japanese Yen*
KRW	South Korean Won
MXN	Mexican Peso
NOK	Norwegian Krone*
PLN	Polish Zloty
RUB	Russian Ruble
SEK	Swedish Krone*
CHF	Swiss Franc*
THB	Thai Baht
TRY	Turkish Lira
USD	United States Dollar*

Hotels

AC	Air conditioning
AI or ALL INCL	All-inclusive (price includes accommodation and all food, drink and activities)
BB	Bed & breakfast (price includes accommodation and breakfast only)
DBL	Double room
DLX	Deluxe room
FB	Full board (price includes accommodation and all meals)
HB	Half board (price includes accommodation, breakfast and evening meal)
HTL	Hotel
NTS	Nights
RO	Room only (price for accommodation only)
SC	Self-catering accommodation
SGL	Single room
STD	Standard room
TRPL	Triple room
TWN	Twin room
TWNB	Twin room with bath
TWNS	Twin room with shower
WC	Toilet
YHA	Youth Hostel Association

ISO Country codes

ISO is the widely used international standard. *The ISO two-letter country codes are used for Internet domains

Country	ISO 2-letter code*	ISO 3-letter code
Australia	AU	AUS
Austria	AT	AUT
Bhutan	BT	BTN
Canada	CA	CAN
China	CN	CHN
Costa Rica	CR	CRI
France	FR	FRA
Germany	DE	DEU
India	IN	IND
Italy	IT	ITA
Kenya	KE	KEN
Korea, Republic of	KR	KOR
Malaysia	MY	MYS
Mexico	MX	MEX
New Zealand	NZ	NZL
Peru	PE	PER
Poland	PL	POL
Russia	RU	RUS
Spain	ES	ESP
Thailand	TH	THA
Turkey	TR	TUR
United Kingdom	GB	GBR
United States	US	USA

Air travel

ARR	Arrival
ATC	Air traffic control
DEP	Departure
ETA	Estimated time of arrival
ETD	Estimated time of departure
ID	Identification
LCC	Low-cost carrier
OW	One-way
RT	Return (Br Eng), Round trip (Am Eng)
SOP	Standard operating procedure
TRSF	Transfer

World's busiest airports
(by international passenger traffic)

LHR	London Heathrow Airport, UK
DXB	Dubai International Airport, United Arab Emirates
HKG	Hong Kong International Airport, Hong Kong
CDG	Paris Charles de Gaulle Airport, France
SIN	Singapore Changi Airport, Singapore
FRA	Frankfurt Airport, Germany
AMS	Amsterdam Airport Schiphol, Netherlands
BKK	Suvarnabhumi Airport, Thailand
ICN	Incheon International Airport, South Korea
NRT	Narita International Airport, Tokyo, Japan

Most visited cities in the world

PAR	Paris
LON	London
BKK	Bangkok
SIN	Singapore
KUL	Kuala Lumpur
NYC	New York
DXB	Dubai
IST	Istanbul
HKG	Hong Kong
SHA	Shanghai

E-mail and letters

ASAP	As soon as possible
BTW	By the way
FYI	For your information
CC	Carbon copy (when a copy of a letter is sent to more than one person)
ENC.	Enclosure (when other papers are included with a letter)
PS	Postscript (when you want to add something after you've finished and signed it)
RSVP	Please reply

Business/Other terms

4Ps	The marketing mix: product, price, promotion, place
7Ps	The extended marketing mix: product, price, promotion, place, people, processes, physical evidence
LEED	Leadership in Energy & Environmental Design standards
SWOT	Strengths, Weaknesses, Opportunities, Threats analysis

Technology

Apps	Applications
CCTV	Closed circuit television
QR code	Quick response code
WI-FI	Wireless fidelity

AUDIO SCRIPT

Unit 1

1.1

1 realized
2 launched
3 survived
4 proved
5 integrated
6 reached
7 provided
8 started

1.2

J = Joe, L = Lucy

J So, Lucy, how's the research trip going?
L Great! Bali is such a beautiful island but it's hard work at the same time.
J Yes, I've been on several trips myself. So, what recommendations have you got so far?
L Well, I think we can offer two alternative holidays – one for adventure tourists and one for families.
J OK, good – go ahead and tell me about them.
L Well, for adventure tourists we can offer hiking and camping holidays on Mount Batur – it's really magnificent. But it can be dangerous as it's an active volcano. But when you get to the top you have the view of sparkling Lake Batur. Plus you get there along the winding roads, full of bends and hills – it's a very exciting drive. And on the way there are lots of isolated villages to visit.
J That sounds very attractive for adventure tourists. What about families? Did you find anything?
L How does this sound: deserted white sand beaches, sea views and a good mix of accommodation choices – bed and breakfast to luxury hotels with spacious rooms.
J Sounds great, where is it? Denpasar? Kuta beach?
L No, it's actually in the north – it's Lovina.
J Good, we'll put together the brochure when you get back. When is your flight back?

1.3

E = Eve, M = Matt

E Look, Matt, the total expenses for the last stag party …
M Yes?
E Well, we didn't make our profit margin.
M What, no way. We never lose on the stag parties.
E Well, this time we did.
M How much are we down?
E About 10%.
M That doesn't sound right to me, Eve. Can we go over the invoices?
E Sure, I have them here for you.
M OK, the flight should have been £534 and the invoice says?
E £534.
M And the airport transfer?
E That was £150.
M That's correct, too. I wonder where the loss came from. What about the tours?

E Well, the total for the canal tour for 12 people was £120 and for the five people who went to Ajax stadium it was £75.
M Which five people?
E The five people who went to the stadium.
M Hang on a minute: that makes 17 people in the group. The trips were booked at the same time, so either no one went to the stadium or five went to the stadium and only seven were on the canal trip.
E I was at the stadium with the group, so the canal tour invoice is wrong. It should be £70. I'll contact them after our meeting and tell them they've charged us too much.
M What about the hotel? How much was that?
E The total bill is £972.
M Is that after the 20% discount?
E That's what it says, but it doesn't sound right. Let me do a quick check. The full amount should have been £1080, and with a 20% discount that would be £864.
M Not £972 – that's only a 10% discount. Would you mind calling the hotel, too?
E I'll get onto it immediately.
M And the other invoice for the nightclub?
E It's £162 after the discount.
M That's fine then. So, what is our profit margin in the end?
E Hang on … it's … 17.6%.
M Not bad – better than a 10% loss. Now, we need to make sure that we have a refund on the invoices that are wrong. And check through all the other tours, too, please. By the end of tomorrow.
E But it's Sunday tomorrow!

Unit 2

2.1

L = Linda, H = Heather

L Heather, I'm travelling down to London tomorrow for the UK Tourism Exhibition and wanted to know the best way to go down. How did you travel when you went last year?
H I thought about catching an early morning flight to London City airport.
L But you didn't fly?
H No, flying was relatively expensive and there were frequent delays because of the air traffic control strike.
L So you drove?
H No, too far in one day. I took the overnight sleeper – the Caledonian sleeper.
L Oh, really, that's unusual.
H Yes, but it's great. It's basically a moving hotel. You can avoid the traffic congestion in the city and accidents on the motorway.
L It's almost a door-to-door service.
H Well, it's not exactly a door-to-door service – you've got to get to the station – but it's easy and painless.
L So if it's an overnight train, it must take about eight hours.

H Not quite as long as that, it's more like six. You go to sleep in Edinburgh and wake up in London. It's a very low stress form of transport. I'd recommend it to anyone.

2.2

A 1 motorway
2 roundabout
3 stopover
4 carriageway
5 comfortable
B 1 expensive
2 equipment
3 compartment
4 unpacking
5 departure

2.3

Thank you all for coming today. My name's Alicia Markova from CSM Customer Service Training and I've been invited to talk about how to make improvements to your service. As a budget airline, I understand you've been getting some tough comments about your service, so I'm here today to look at the problems and suggest some solutions. So here's my first suggestion: know what your problems are!

I'm going to talk about the results of a survey which compared budget airlines with scheduled airlines. When passengers were asked what they didn't like most about travelling on budget airlines, they said: uncomfortable seating. 53% of passengers stated this as the main problem for budget airlines in contrast to scheduled airlines where only 23% mentioned this as the problem. Unfortunately, more seats per plane is built into the budget airline business model but we can let passengers know that what they lose in comfort, they gain in low fares.

The second problem was the hidden costs in the ticket – 44% of passengers identified this as a problem for the budget airlines, but only 16% said the same for scheduled airlines. The answer here is more transparency: let the passenger know the full costs before they buy, with a list of charges.

The next thing passengers disliked was the in-flight food – 37% for budget airlines but only 12% for scheduled airlines. The cost of in-flight food is passed on to the passenger, so you could introduce a more expensive menu for passengers who want better food.

So far, I haven't mentioned the problem of air rage and badly behaved passengers: this was the fourth problem, at 32% for budget airlines but just 11% for scheduled airlines. In-flight crew need training in dealing with badly behaved passengers.

Finally, passengers were unhappy about the price – and this is probably connected to point 2. 31% of passengers say that budget airlines are not that cheap. However, 41% say that scheduled airlines are expensive. Again, we can let passengers know that the price of the fare really depends on their choices.

As we can see from the table, there are some things that we can't do anything about – for example, not enough seat space – but other things we can improve.

Unit 3

3.1

Hello and welcome to the Japan Guide podcast. We're looking this week at one of Japan's more interesting places to stay: the capsule hotel. Capsule hotels are inspired by efficient use of space and functional comfort and they could only have been invented in one country – Japan. People can stay here overnight in a cheap room. The hotel consists of two sections: a public section with lounge and communal bathing and a private section with sleeping capsules and lockers. Each capsule, or pod, is 2 metres long, 1.25 metres wide and 80 centimetres high – this is where you sleep. Because there is little room for anything else, you have to store your clothes and belongings in a locker, which is 130 centimetres high, 26 centimetres wide and 48 centimetres deep. A capsule hotel is open all the time so you can book in any time. However, checkout is at 10 a.m. and you have to leave then, or pay an extra 500 yen per 30 minutes. Capsule hotels are most frequently used by Japanese business people after a long day at work but are also ideal for backpackers who haven't got much money. Men and women have strictly separate areas – no mixed rooms here. Night clothes are provided in the locker by the hotel and visitors are strongly encouraged to wear these for reasons of hygiene and comfort.

3.2

2 metres long
1.25 metres wide
80 centimetres high
130 centimetres high
26 centimetres wide
48 centimetres deep

3.3

J =Jorge, W = Wanju
J Good evening. Welcome to the Hotel Concordia.
W Hi, I'm booked in for tonight.
J Can I take your name?
W Chang, Wanju Chang.
J OK, let me see. Erm, nope. You're not booked in tonight.
W But that's impossible. I booked the room over a month ago.
J Not with us. I don't have anything down here for you. Are you sure you booked with us, madam?
W Is this the Hotel Concordia?
J Well, that's what it said on the sign outside last time I looked.
W Then I booked a room here.
J Erm, no, you didn't. There's no room booking for you on the system.
W I'm not interested in your system – I booked a room last month, and someone called Elena Mata took the booking.
J Oh, Elena, you shouldn't have booked a room with her – she's completely unreliable.

W Well, that's who took the booking.
J Look, we're full tonight so I suggest you try the Servisotel on the other side of the city and come back tomorrow when we're a bit quieter. In the meantime, I'll make a note of your complaint and let the boss know what happened so that it doesn't happen again.
W This is completely unacceptable!

3.4

J = Jorge, W = Wanju
J Good evening. Welcome to the Hotel Concordia.
W Hi, I'm booked in for tonight.
J Can I take your name?
W Chang, Wanju Chang.
J OK, let me see. I'm sorry, madam, we don't seem to have a booking for you tonight.
W But that's impossible. I booked the room over a month ago.
J Oh, let me check again. … I'm sorry about this, but I'm afraid we don't have you booked in tonight but we have a booking for you for tomorrow night.
W Well, someone called Elena Mata took the booking.
J We don't usually make mistakes with our room bookings but I'll look into it right away for you.
W OK, thank you.
    …
J Well, Ms Chang, I've contacted Elena and she remembers the telephone conversation – you're from Taipei, aren't you?
W Yes, that's correct.
J There seem to have been some problems with our new room reservation system – just one or two but unfortunately, this is another one. So, I'll record it and pass it on to our IT services to make sure they know about it.
W That's fine, but what about my booking?
J Well, I've done everything I possibly can. Fortunately, we've had a cancellation for tonight. We can offer you that room at a reduced rate and move you to your original room tomorrow night.
W Well, I guess that's OK.
J If you don't mind, I'll ask the manager tomorrow to check that you were satisfied with your room.
W OK, fine. Thanks.

Unit 4

4.1

1
   So, temperatures this weekend running about 50 degrees Fahrenheit, which is above average. Our warm winter continues in a drizzly New York this Friday. Sunny intervals take the temperature to a high of 55 degrees Fahrenheit over Atlantic City, where we'll see fine weather. Further north in Monticello we'll have light rain with temperatures at a cooler 40 degrees. The overall picture – it's going to cool down this weekend with the warm front giving way to cold air and changeable conditions.

2
   Well, we've got cloud cover over New York City for Saturday and it's been around all night long, giving us temperatures around 41 degrees Fahrenheit. So that's warm but cloudy over New York, and further south it's looking changeable and unsettled at 52 degrees. That's mainly due to a tropical storm over the sea, giving Atlantic City some thundery showers. In the Monticello region, temperatures are still above average at 37 degrees Fahrenheit, but there's heavy rain here as a cold front comes down from the north.
3
   Take your umbrella this Sunday, folks – there are scattered showers moving up from the south following yesterday's stormy weather in Atlantic City from tropical storm Rico. It's 48 degrees Fahrenheit in Central Park and mostly cloudy over New York City. In Atlantic City itself, we've still got a few thundery showers hanging on with temperatures falling again today to 45 degrees. And that cold front coming down from the north over Monticello is moving south, causing strong winds and light snow showers in the region, with temperatures at just 35 degrees Fahrenheit.

4.2

G = Gillian, D = Denise Gee
G Hello, Mrs Gee, please take a seat.
D Thanks.
G Now, have you had any more thoughts about this year's holiday since we last spoke?
D Well, we talked about it last night and we've got a better idea of what we want.
G OK, let's start with dates. When would you like to go?
D August the 13th for a fortnight, until the 27th.
G OK – for three people?
D No, my husband, our daughters – Kate and Elaine – and myself are going.
G Do you have any ideas where you'd like to go?
D Yes – somewhere hot and not too far.
G So, probably Europe.
D We were thinking of the Mediterranean – Spain, Turkey, Greece – somewhere not too expensive.
G OK, we've got a good range of products in that region. What's your price range for this holiday?
D We're thinking of spending around £3,000.
G I'm sure we can arrange something for you. Tell me what kind of holiday you had in mind.
D Nothing special, really. Bill and I are quite happy sitting on a beach reading.
G So, a beach holiday – sand, sea and sunshine.
D Yes, somewhere safe where we can keep an eye on the children but at the same time give them a bit of freedom. The girls are growing up now and need things to interest them.
G What kind of things are they interested in?
D They're quite active.
G So you'd need a place with activities like volleyball or surfing.

D I'm afraid that's a bit too grown up for them – they're eight and ten. But they love horses and swimming.

G Then you'll need a place with a pool.

D Yes, it's important to have a pool, and play activities. And possibly pony trekking or horse-riding.

G OK.

D Do you think we'll get somewhere with all that?

G I think we're looking at a resort hotel or a holiday village. We've got a good range of choices at the moment. What other things would you like? For example, evening entertainment – dancing, music, cinema …

D We both like going to see films – a cinema would be great – but we couldn't leave the children alone.

G So, you would need a childminding service so you and your husband can relax a bit without the children.

D That would be a real plus. I don't know that we would use it really but it would be nice to have the option.

G And what about the services? Would you want fully catered, part catered or self-catering?

D Fully catered. There's no way I'm cooking on my holiday – I do all the cooking at home.

G I understand where you're coming from there, believe me! OK, then, leave it with me and I'll get back to you tomorrow with a couple of suggestions. Do we have your email address?

4.3

1 one thousand two hundred
2 thirty five thousand, two hundred and fifty-seven
3 eight hundred and twenty-five thousand
4 one million eight hundred and thirty thousand
5 one billion seven hundred and ninety million
6 one and a half trillion

4.4

P = Presenter, R = Robert, W = Winifred

P Hello and welcome to *The Debate* – the show where we discuss the week's important issues. At the start of this week's budget debate in parliament, Tourism Minister Robert Manson announced expected growth in the sector at a time of economic gloom. Mr Manson joins us today. Hello, Minister.

R Hello.

P But this isn't good news for everyone. The opposition's environmental expert Winifred Rodney isn't happy – and she's in the studio with us, too. Good evening, Ms Rodney.

W Good evening.

P Now, Mr Manson, I understand you have big plans for Jamaica's tourist industry.

R Yes, we have the wonderful opportunity of encouraging the development of two new luxury resorts in the Montego Bay area at a cost of $5.5 million, which will bring work to around 2,500 people.

P Why would a development company choose Jamaica, not Trinidad or Cuba?

R We've got two key advantages over those places – an experienced workforce and a well-established tourism industry. Foreign companies know they are welcome here and can find people to work with.

P Ms Rodney – something to be welcomed, surely?

W Of course, we have a high unemployment rate and any jobs are welcome. But 20% of our economy is based on tourism. Tourism is a benefit and threat to Jamaica – as our other industries decline, the economy becomes unbalanced. In addition, we have two major weaknesses. First of all, our power network is very old and power cuts are happening more and more often to ordinary people as we try to keep the big hotels supplied with electricity.

P That's true. Minister?

W If I may continue. The second weakness is water supply – the big resorts use a lot of water for swimming pools, golf courses, laundry and so on.

R Yes, but we have to deal with these things – we're in a competitive area and have long-term threats from developing destinations like Cuba. Plus our own short-term social problems – social unrest caused by unemployment and the high murder rate – also threaten growth. We can use the income generated by tourism to cut unemployment and invest in electricity and water supplies.

W As I said, I'm not against tourism but let's look at the other opportunities open to us – not just big new developments like Montego Bay. Why can't we have more eco-tourism projects where visitors stay with local people and don't damage the environment? Let me ask the minister – how much money is being invested in these small-scale projects?

Unit 5

5.1

1

Now we come to the main part of the exhibition – if you'll just follow me through this way. And here we are, ladies and gentlemen, one of the greatest medieval works of art – the Bayeux tapestry. Before we start – can everyone hear me OK? Good. Right, the tapestry was started in the 1070s after the Battle of Hastings on October 14th, 1016, I think, or was it 1066? Now I remember – in 1066. Anyway, it tells the story of an epic battle during which England's King Harold was killed and the Norman conquest of England began. The magnificent tapestry is 70 metres long and 50 centimetres high and tells the story in 58 vivid scenes. If you look closely, you'll see the main characters – here is King Harold and over here is William the Conqueror. Or is that King Harold and this William? Never mind. The tapestry was rediscovered in 1725 and moved here in 1983.

2

At the National Gallery in Oslo our most famous painting is by Edvard Munch and it is, of course, The Scream. So, if you'd like to gather round … Can everyone hear me? Over at the back – can you hear me OK? OK? Good, then I'll start. The painting is famous for its bold colours, sweeping brush strokes and as a portrait of emotional intensity. In fact, the painting, finished in 1893, was one of the first Expressionist paintings – an artistic movement which was a reaction in part to Impressionism. As you can see, it's not the size of the painting which makes it powerful – it's only 91 centimetres by 74 centimetres – it's the colours and the expression of the central figure. You may not know this, but the painting was stolen in February 1994 and recovered again in the same year in March. Now we keep a close eye on it – so if you move this way, we'll take a look at …

3

Hello, everyone, and thank you for coming today – it's a bit chilly in the park but there are two advantages when the weather is as cold as this: first, you get this beautiful winter light. Second, no one else wants to come out in the cold so we'll get a good, uninterrupted look at the exhibits. First, we're going to look at the work of one of the most famous women sculptors in the world – Barbara Hepworth. Just in front of us is one of her greatest sculptures, Family of Man, completed in 1970. Barbara was born in 1903 at a time when sculpture was about the human form. But Barbara became more interested in the materials she was carving – stone, wood and bronze. Eventually, Barbara moved away from realism altogether and produced abstract sculptures characterized by bold shapes, with circles carved out of them to introduce light.

5.2

1 1729
2 2011
3 February, 1994
4 November, 2002
5 October the 14th, 1066
6 The 15th of January, 1961

5.3

C = Claire, D = Dieter

C Hi, I'm calling from New Jersey European tours. I've been reading your brochure and itinerary of the Sounds of Classical Germany tour. It's very interesting, and it's something we're interested in promoting, but I wanted to check some details with you.

D Sure, go ahead.

C The programme looks good – great choice of composers and venues – love the brochure, too.

D Thank you very much.

C How big is Germany? I mean – what's the drive time between locations?

D Well, Berlin to Dresden is just two hours. But Dresden to Bonn is a bit further – It's six and a quarter hours.

C Wow, that's a lot of gas.

D Yes, it does add to the cost. Are the journey times a problem?

C No, not really, but our main customers are quite elderly and long journeys tend to tire them. You know, after an eight-hour bus ride, these guys want to see a bed, not a concert.

D I see.

C Can I ask you about these optional tickets?

D Go ahead.

C First of all, just how much are they? How much is the Tuesday night at the opera?

D Well, a concert at the Semper Opera will be €166.

C €166, I see, and what about the Beethoven chamber music on Thursday?

D That's just €20.

C Well, that's a bargain. What about the Saturday night at the Festspielhaus in Beyreuth?

D It's €270 per person. We strongly recommend that customers take this option as it's the second part of the opera.

C OK. And then the coach to Munich takes …?

D It's just two hours twenty minutes.

C Uh-huh.

D Do you have any concerns?

C Well, my main concern is the total price at €2,550.00 per person – it's a bit on the high side for most of my customers.

D I see.

C But when you add in all the optional extras, the total bill comes in at, in US dollars … at nearly $4,000, you know. Can you get a discount from the concert organizers?

D Well, we've kept the price as low as possible considering all the overheads involved, and it's very difficult to negotiate a discount with the concert organizers as so many people want to attend these concerts.

C Sure, but what I'm saying is that if we can include the optional extras and get a price nearer to $3,700, we could probably bring in more customers.

D A $300 reduction will be very difficult to achieve. Would you be willing to reduce your rate of commission? And perhaps we could send you a customized itinerary? Then perhaps …

Unit 6

6.1

C = Chairman , A = Angelica

C Welcome back, everyone, to the Republic of Equatorial Guinea Tourism Consultation Committee. To help us today, we have Angelica N'Dour, from the Pro-poor Tourism Association.

A Thank you for inviting me. I know that the committee has been thinking about encouraging mass tourism by developing more big, new tourist resorts along the coast like the international luxury resort of Sipopo. Sipopo certainly attracts attention and raises the profile of the country – but are more of these resorts really what Equatorial Guinea needs? I'd like to consider a pro-poor tourism approach, where the benefits to the poor are greater than the costs. Developing niche tourism is one way of doing this. First, let me ask the committee two questions: how much money do these big luxury resorts bring in to the country and how sustainable is this programme?

C Perhaps you could tell us, Angelica?

A Welcoming foreign tourism companies to Equatorial Guinea has major benefits – professional knowledge, economies of scale – but mass tourism has disadvantages, too. The first disadvantage is about real income for the country. Direct income from tourism is the money that stays in the destination country. Now, for a package tour, about 80 % of the income stays out of the country. It's estimated that from every US $100 spent on a vacation, only around US $5 actually stays in the country's economy. This is what tourist industry analysts call 'leakage'.

C I see, so we don't get as much income as we would like. And your second issue?

A Sustainability. Mass tourism uses resources which are already in short supply – for example, a single golf course can use as much water as a town of 10,000 people. People come in to tourist areas to work and so need a place to live, and this causes inflation in prices.

C I see. So what we get from mass tourism may not be as much as we think, and of course the little we do get is spent on the infrastructure for the resorts.

A Yes, that's right.

C So, what about niche tourism, then? Can you tell us more about that?

A Niche tourists tend to stay longer and this helps to develop real skills in the community. They also spend more in the local economy and niche tour operators can charge a higher price for these kinds of specialist holiday, too. But pro-poor tourism isn't just about niche tourism – it's much wider and can involve mass tour operators. Tour operators can help to improve the wages of local people and can allow local business greater access to hotels. Finally, they can invest in training local people and involve them in decision-making.

6.2

1 1.5 million
2 107 dollars
3 715
4 2 out of 5
5 20 per cent
6 three quarters
7 13 per cent
8 130

6.3

Hello and welcome to *Tourist Talk*, where today I'm looking at a kind of niche tourism – festival tourism. In the UK there are over 200 music festivals taking place all over the country during summer. There are an increasing number of multi-million-pound festivals like the Isle of Wight festival, Glastonbury and T in the Park, which attract international pop stars and hundreds of thousands of music fans. Recently, we have seen 'boutique' festivals aimed at attracting the music fans who went to festivals in the 1970s and want to repeat the experience with their families. These festivals are smaller – 5,000 to 35,000 people – and have a wider variety of events, including art and theatre as well as music. Some of the larger festivals are massive and the money spent locally can be massive too. The Isle of Wight Council estimates £10 million of income just from festival visitors. T in the Park brought in £7.3 million for Scotland and festival goers at Glastonbury made up one seventh of the yearly £180 million income from tourism activity in the region. While clean-up operations cost the local council growing amounts of money, the benefits to tourism in the area are also increasing. Hotels can be full to capacity and the image of the town or region benefits. After all, the Isle of Wight was recently named by a leading style magazine as one of the most fashionable places to visit in Europe, alongside Morocco and Sicily.

Unit 7

7.1

1 What shall we do tomorrow? I'm getting a bit bored sitting on the beach. Why don't we go to look at the Ifugao rice terraces? They're a really authentic part of Philippine life and it would make a change to see something like that.

2 We'd always wanted to visit here but we really wanted to understand what we were looking at – you know. So many people go to these prestigious heritage sites and just don't understand the significance of what they're looking at. That's why we took night classes about Cambodia's religious history before we came to Angkor Watt.

3 I'm not particularly interested in cultural heritage but I was surprised by how much I enjoyed my visit to Ayutthaya, the ancient capital of Thailand. We came to Bangkok for a week and Ayutthaya was part of a one-day tour. I didn't expect to like any archaeological sites but I was really impressed and feel really lucky that I went.

4 What's next on the tour? Let's see – the Great Wall of China, made to protect the Chinese people. That sounds really quaint! We've got two hours there and then we're going back to Beijing. Is there a souvenir shop? I love shopping for gifts.

5 We have family here in India and we like to take long holidays to experience our cultural heritage. We like to see as many world heritage sites as possible, like the Taj Mahal. It's such a beautiful building despite its sad purpose – the burial place of the Emperor's dead wife.

7.2

T = Tom , M = Morgan, P = Pilar

T Morning, everyone. Let's make a start, shall we? So, what happened then, Morgan?

M What do you mean, Tom?

T I mean, ticket sales of £15,000 against expected sales of £75,000, head office saying that the Arts Festival organizers are very unhappy with our marketing, publicity for the festival one month late. That's what I mean, Morgan.

M Ah, well – I don't know why you're ask …

T Why I'm asking?

M No, I don't know why you're asking me. It was Pilar's job.

T Pilar, do you have anything to say?

P What? Morgan's saying I'm responsible!

M Well, I did put you in charge of the Arts Festival account.

7.3

**C = Carol, S = Silvia, G = Gunther,
T = Trevor**

C Morning, Silvia, Gunther, Trevor.

S Morning, Carol.

G/T Morning.

C Did you have time to look at the agenda? OK, good. We're here to talk about planning for the festival. As you know, our competitors lost the contract after last year. Shall we begin?

All Sure / Yes / Fine.

C The first item on the agenda is the size of the festival. Gunther?

G The festival proper begins in August but there's the fringe festival before that which attracts around 250,000 visitors – so arguably, the fringe festival is bigger than the actual festival.

S That's a lot of people.

G Yes, but the festival organizers want to expand it to 400,000 to rival the Edinburgh Festival.

T That will mean a lot of shows.

G Yes, they'll need to expand their team by 50%. And go from 35,000 performances to 45,000.

C Silvia, do you have anything to add?

S Yes, Carol – they're spending a lot of money to make this happen, over £1.25 million.

G And almost one third of that is on advertising – that's a lot of money, too! Personally, I think we should plan to market for half a million people, not just the expected 400,000. That way, we can make sure the organizers are happy and we keep the contract.

C OK. Do I take it we're all in agreement with Gunther?

S/T Yes, of course / Definitely.

C Can we move on to the next item, then? Timing. Trevor, what do you think?

T Timing is absolutely crucial. That's why the last company lost the contract – they were late with the marketing.

C So, what do we need?

T Well, they want 1.5 million leaflets sending out by direct mail marketing.

C I'm sure we can handle that.

T Yes, I'll deal with that, no problem.

C Good. I think we've covered everything, then. Excellent. Is there any other business?

7.4

1 Do you have anything to say?
2 Shall we begin?
3 Do you have anything to add?
4 Can we move on to the next item, then?
5 Is there any other business?

Unit 8

8.1

H = Hotelier, HI = Hotel inspector

H So, how did the Juice Bar do this year, inspector?

HI Well, let's go over the results. Last year the Juice Bar scored only 10 for greeting guests, very poor. This year was not perfect but better, and it scored 40 – so that's a massive 300% improvement.

H Oh, good. And was the waitress more helpful than last year?

HI No, not really – she got a 20 for that again. She still couldn't even tell me what was in one of the cocktails, the Dragon Cocktail.

H That's easy – dragon fruit and pineapple.

HI Exactly.

H Oh, dear. And could you get the drink you ordered?

HI Yes – there was very good availability, I gave 50 for that again.

H And speed?

H Again, the service was excellent and got 50. That's a 25% improvement on last year.

H OK. What about her appearance? Was it better this year?

HI Yes – a 66% improvement, in fact. She was tidy and smart so she got another 50.

H So, overall?

H Overall, last year the Juice Bar scored 150, which meant that it was average. But things are much better this year.

H Great. So what's the new score and percentage improvement?

HI The total score is 210, an overall good. It works out at an improvement of 78%, so well done!

8.2

First of all, thank you for inviting me to the Howatt Hotel. Before I start, I want to read out some of the answers I got from our online survey – you remember I asked you to complete them last week? So, 'How do you feel about giving presentations?' One person wrote: 'I feel terrible, I can't sleep the night before a presentation.' Another

wrote: 'I hate presentations. I hate giving them and I hate going to them.' Well, the title of today's presentation is 'Presenting effectively' and my name is Sue Dawson from Staff Training Events. People think of presentations as formal events and maybe that's why they get nervous or hate them. But in fact we give mini-presentations all the time – when we're explaining things to other people, passing on information or teaching someone about something.

We can divide presentations into three basic parts – before, during and after – and in this talk I'll look at each of these parts. What you do before your presentation is the key to how well your presentation goes on the day. Some people think they can just turn up to a place and give a presentation – they're the poor presenters who make you hate going to presentations. With presentations, preparation is everything. The most important thing is to think about your audience – what do they want to know and what do they already know? Passing on information in an interesting way is key to your presentation. Secondly, before you go into your presentation, practise and rehearse as much as you can. You'll feel much more confident on the day of your presentation if you've prepared well.

The next stage of the presentation I'll talk about is during the presentation. Always start by greeting the audience – it's an obvious point but you'd be surprised at how many presenters start without saying hello, or who they are and which organization they are from. Once you have the attention of the audience, you need to keep it. Don't be tempted to digress – stick to your plan. And remember – a presentation is to give information, not to entertain people. The best way to keep your audience interested is to make sure you're telling them what they want to know, clearly. You need a clear structure to guide your audience through the presentation. Start by telling them what you're going to tell them. Then tell them. Finally, tell your audience what you have said. Before the presentation, you have prepared well and rehearsed a lot – so now you can be confident and natural. Don't rush, and try to talk about each slide for about two minutes.

This brings me to my next point. Don't put too much text on each slide. Slides should contain the main points only, not the content of your presentation. And never read from the slides or turn your back to the audience – keep good eye contact and good body language.

Finally, when your presentation is over, make sure you invite your audience to ask questions. Deal with questions calmly and clearly. Now, you may get some stupid questions but don't be impolite. Say something like: 'That's an interesting question but it's outside the scope of my presentation' or 'Perhaps we could talk about it later.' Don't forget to give out photocopies of your slides or any other marketing material you have.

So, thank you for listening. We've covered the main points of giving presentations – preparation, what to do during the presentation and questions at the end. Now do you have any questions? Yes, Philippa …?

8.3

A 1 confident
  2 interesting
  3 finally
B 1 presenter
  2 effective
  3 impression
C 1 presentation
  2 information
  3 preparation

8.4

INT = Interviewer, MR = Mr Roche, MG = Ms Gonzalez, MY = Ms Yeboah

INT So, Mr Roche, can you tell us what improvements there have been since our report on the hotel?
MR My favourite recommendation was for the manager to do their own job, not everyone else's. But the best recommendation was making some of the staff into team leaders, and this has been very good. Now, when you want something done, you don't have to wait for someone to say yes or no. You can go straight to the team leader and get an answer. For example, before, if you saw a really dirty room and you knew it was going to take a lot longer than 50 minutes to clean, you had to ask the boss. Now, we ask the team leader to send another cleaner to help. Much more efficient.
INT Hello again, Ms Gonzalez. Can you tell us what has changed at the hotel since we last interviewed you?
MR I'm still front-of-house at the reception desk or working at the back of reception on room bookings, so no changes there. We have a new team leader – and that's more efficient. It gives us more flexibility to arrange our work schedule. But the manager! He just can't keep away from the main foyer. Greeting guests, giving the porter orders, telling reception what to do, telling the waiters what to do. We have team leaders for that now and being told your job every day is really bad for morale. That was the recommendation I liked best – for the boss not to interfere – but he just can't stay in his office.
INT So, Ms Yeboah, can you tell us how things have changed since our report?
MY Well, I'm still head housekeeper and some things have got better but some things are still the same. The boss still comes to the office and tells my cleaners what to do. But now we're organized into teams so that's much more efficient. But my favourite recommendation was for staff training. That's made a big difference to morale and motivation. For example,

before, we didn't get much training but now we've got a hotel training manager and she's given staff a training programme. That's great.

Unit 9

9.1

J = Jan , B = Barry

J Hello, my name's Jan, calling from Travelogue customer services.
B Oh, hello.
J I understand you've just come back from your holiday. Would you mind if I asked you a few questions?
B No, not at all.
J Thanks. OK, first question. Could you tell me where you went?
B We went to Italy.
J Did you enjoy your holiday?
B Yes, yes, very much. And we learnt so much about Italian cookery.
J Oh, that sounds really interesting. Where did you get the idea for your holiday?
B We were watching a TV holiday programme and we saw a similar holiday during the break. There was an advert by Relax and Do Holidays. So we searched for the company on the internet and found it quite easily.
J So, what was special about the holiday?
B Well, we love food and cooking, and it seemed like a great idea to combine our holiday with learning some new skills. So we looked around and saw the holiday at the cookery school in Tuscany.
J Ah, I see. And could you tell me where you bought the holiday?
B Actually, we bought it at our local travel agent's. We wanted to get more information on this kind of specialist holiday and our travel agent is very good.
J Did you go to the travel agent to book it?
B Yes. Sometimes talking to someone face-to-face is essential in helping you decide. I think our agent is trying to establish himself in this area – probably can't compete with the big agents.
J And did you shop around for similar products? Can I ask if you looked at the competition?
B This kind of holiday is unique, so you can't really compare. The prices the competition charges don't really affect your choice, so we didn't shop around
J Do you think the holiday was good value?
B Oh, yes, definitely.
J Would you mind telling me if you got a discount?
B Remember, we went to talk to the local travel agent?
J Yes.
B Well, he got us an early-booking discount – you know what I mean, book six months ahead and you get 10% reduction.
J Right. So, could you tell me how you would rate your holiday – on a scale of 1–5 where 5 is excellent?

B Well, our travel agent was great and the holiday was excellent, so I would give it a 5, definitely.
J Good. Well, thank you very much for your time!
B My pleasure.

9.2

A/P = Answerphone , E = Eddie

A

A/P Welcome to Marine Leisure Services. All our operators are busy at the moment. Your call is very important to us, so please leave a message and we'll get back to you as soon as possible.
E Hi, it's Eddie – can you pass on a message to Rita? I'm stuck in traffic at the moment so I'm going to be late bringing the new brochures through. I know she wanted them urgently, so could she ring me on 0777 482 9635 and I can let her know how long I'll be. Bye for now.

A/A = Automated answer, H = Hans, S = Sandra

B

A/A To help us deal with your enquiry, please choose from the following three options. For reservations, please press 1, to book at the hotel restaurant, press 2, to speak to the main desk, it's 3, and for any other business, press 5.
S Hello, Sandra here, how can I help you?
H My name's Hans Gert. I'd like to book a room, please.
S Oh, I'm sorry, sir, you've come through to the wrong department – we're the restaurant. Hold on a moment and I'll put you through to room bookings. Just in case we're cut off, let me take your number so we can get back to you if necessary.
H Sure – it's 49 22 1 7897650.
S Let me read that back to you – 49 – that's Germany, isn't it? – 22 1 7897650
H Yes, that's correct.

S/T = Seattle Taxis, E = Erica

C

S/T Hello, Seattle Taxis.
E Hi, my name's Erica Wong. I think I left my bag in the back of one of your cars.
S/T When did you take the taxi?
E About 2.30 this afternoon – from Central station to 42, 77th Avenue.
S/T Don't worry – I'll look into it for you. What number are you calling from?
E I'm on Seattle 33 95 874.
S/T Right – and your email?
E ericaw@qmail.com
S/T OK, maam, leave it with us. I'll sort it out for you and get back to you later today.

A = Angie, F = Frank

D

A Look, Frank, my phone's running out of money – I'll call you back after I've topped it up.
F No, don't ring me back – just hang up now and go on video chat.
A Good idea – what's your video chat name?
F FTurgut007.
A 007?
F Yes – what's yours?

A Angie55. I'll look for you now and call soon. OK?
F Fine – speak soon.

9.3

1 0444 482 9635
2 36 1 3368511
3 00 44 141 3336655
4 w.stanley@zmail.com
5 LiPeng50

Unit 10

10.1

My manager … her name's Verity … she's very keen on team building. Verity believes that we don't work as a team so one day she organized a team-building away day. Two days before that, an advert had come to the office for Incentivize and Verity knew at once that they were the right people for us.

We had a choice of paintballing, rafting or bungee-jumping. We all chose rafting and then Incentivize told us that their instructor hadn't passed her health and safety test so we couldn't do that. Our second choice was paintballing. On a cold, rainy day, we ended up in the middle of a forest in the countryside, freezing and wishing we were in bed. Early that morning, an old bus had picked us up at the office and taken us there. Unfortunately, it stopped five kilometres before the paintball area and we had to walk the rest of the way. At the area, Incentivize gave us some old jackets and paintball guns and put us into two teams.

We started at 1:00 but by 1:20 the paintball guns had stopped working. At this point we had had enough and we decided to go back to the office. By the time we had reached the office again, our team had written a long letter of complaint. So I guess the teamwork activity had worked!

10.2

1 Two days before that, an advert had come to the office for Incentivize.
2 Their instructor hadn't passed her health and safety test.
3 Early that morning, an old bus had picked us up at the office.
4 Unfortunately, it stopped five kilometres before the paintball area.
5 By 1:20 the paintball guns had stopped working.
6 So we had to go back to the office.
7 Our team had written a long letter of complaint.
8 So I guess the teamwork activity had worked.

10.3

P = Perry, M = Marta

A

P Excuse me, are you Marta Chaves, by any chance?
M Yes, yes, I am.
P Oh, hello, I don't think we've met before. I'm Perry from the Johannesburg branch.
M Nice to meet you, Perry.
P I must say you look very nice in that dress – very chic.
M Oh, erm, thank you. Erm, there's someone I need to talk to over there. Excuse me.

P = Peter , X = Xiumei

B

P Professor Yang, isn't it?
X Yes, that's right.
P Hello, professor, let me introduce myself. I'm Peter from the Amsterdam office.
X Oh, nice to meet you finally, Peter.
P Yes, what a pity we're meeting for the first time at such a horrible venue.
X What do you mean?
P Well, it's a bit of a dump, isn't it?
X Oh, I thought it was quite nice when I booked it.
P You booked it? Oh, well, not everyone has good taste, do they?

N = Neil , A = Alison

C

N You must be Alison.
A That's right. You're Neil, aren't you?
N Yes. It's good to meet you at last.
A It's nice to put a name to a face at last. Well, what do you think of the new president?
N The president of the company?
A Yes, isn't she awful? No good at all.
N Erm, well it's a little too early to say, really. It's a nice venue for the conference, isn't it?
A Personally, I feel that Bob, the vice president, should have got the job, not an outsider …

J = Justin, L = Luke

D

J Luke, long time, no see.
L Hi, Justin.
J Have you been here long?
L No.
J Did you arrive today?
L Yes.
J Was your journey OK?
L Yes, it was fine.
J Is work OK?
L Yes, thanks.
J Is your family well?
L Yes, they are.

10.4

1 You're Neil, aren't you?
2 It's been a long day, hasn't it?
3 The brochures were here, weren't they?
4 Professor Yang, isn't it?
5 The trip is on Sunday, isn't it?
6 I didn't expect to see Mary here, did you?
7 It's not eight o'clock already, is it?
8 The food's superb, isn't it?

10.5

A

P = Piera, F = Francois,
R = Receptionist, T = Tom

F Look, Piera, I've really enjoyed talking to you but I must rush off now to the seminar on Virtual Marketing.
P Well, why don't we meet up later to continue our conversation?
F That's a great idea.

B

R = Receptionist, P = Piera

R Hello, madam. Can I take your name?
P Hi. I'm Piera Chow. I'm here for three nights.
R Just a moment, Ms Chow. I'll just check your details. OK, I've got the booking right here for you. Room 1412.

C

F = Francois, P = Piera

F So, Piera, is this dish typical in your region?
P Yes, spicy hotpot is a Sichuan speciality. Do you like it?
F It's delicious.
P Not too spicy?

D

P = Piera , F = Francois

P Have you got any plans for dinner this evening?
F I was going to call room service and eat in my room.
P I've got a better idea. How about going out for dinner together? I know a great restaurant not far from the convention centre.

E

T = Tom, P = Piera

T Hi. I was looking through the conference programme and noticed that your company specializes in the same kind of tourism as us.
P I see. My name's Piera Chow. Here's my business card.
T I'm Tom Gross. Here's my card. We've seen good growth in our travel branch of the business.
P Yes, we're quite new to the market – it's an idea that's just come to our country.

F

P = Piera , R = Receptionist

P It feels quite chilly today.
R Yes, I'm afraid it hasn't been very good this week. It's been misty and rainy.
P So, do you think I'll need an umbrella?

Pearson Education Limited
Edinburgh Gate
Harlow
Essex CM20 2JE
England
and Associated Companies throughout the world.

www.pearsonelt.com/tourism

© Pearson Education Limited 2013

First published 2013
Third impression 2023

ISBN: Workbook +Key/Audio CD Pk
9781447923855
Printed by Neografia in Slovakia

Workbook -Key/Audio CD Pk
9781447923862
Printed by Neografia in Slovakia

Set in Avenir Light 9.5/12.5pt

*'DK' and the DK 'open book' logo are trade marks of Dorling Kindersley
Limited and are used in this publication under licence.*

Picture Credits
The publisher would like to thank the following for their kind
permission to reproduce their photographs:

(Key: b-bottom; c-centre; l-left; r-right; t-top)

Alamy Images: Curtseyes 42tr, Gardel Bertrand / Hemis 5br; **DK
Images:** 5bl, Christopher Pillitz 8tr, Joe Cornish 39tr, Nigel Hicks 44tl,
46tl, 53tr; **Fotolia.com:** 12, 14tl, 13, 15tr, 16, 18tl, 17, 19tr, 20, 22tl, 24,
26tl, 25, 27tr, 29, 31tr, 36, 38tl, 37, 39tr, 4, 6tl, 40, 42tl, 5, 7tr, 8, 10tl, 9,
11tr; **Getty Images:** Alistair Berg / Digital Vision 14tr, Jupiterimages 12c,
32tc; **Lonely Planet Images:** Christopher Baker 18b, Tim Barker 17br;
Pearson Education Ltd: 28, 30tl, 32, 34tl; **Rex Features:** Sipa Press 20cr;
Robert Harding World Imagery: Roy Rainford 7cl, Tibor Bognar / age
fotostock 31cl; **Shutterstock.com:** 25tr, 28b, 21, 23tr, 33, 35tr, 41, 43tr;
Sofitel: 24c, 24cr; **SuperStock:** age fotostock 17tr, Ambient Images Inc.
22bl, Travel Library Limited 29cl

Cover images: Front: **4Corners Images:** Franco Cogoli / SIME tc;
Corbis: Blaine Harrington III b; **DK Images:** Paul Young / Departure
Lounge bc; **Getty Images:** Stuart Gregory t; Back: **Getty Images:**
Don Hebert tl; **Robert Harding World Imagery:** Neil Emmerson bl;
SuperStock: DeAgostini cl

All other images © Pearson Education

In some instances we have been unable to trace the owners of copyright
material, and we would appreciate any information that would enable us
to do so.

Illustration Acknowledgements

(Key: b-bottom; c-centre; l-left; r-right; t-top)

Kathy Baxendale 13t, 16l, 21t, 23t, 41t, 58b